DESIGN FOR YOU

DESIGN

JOHN WILEY & SONS, INC.

FOR YOU SECOND EDITION

ETHEL JANE BEITLER
Texas Technological College

BILL LOCKHART
Texas Technological College

New York · London · Sydney · Toronto

Library of Congress Catalog Card Number: 73-76050
SBN 471 06337 1

20 19 18 17 16 15 14 13 12 11

Printed in the United States of America

Dedicated to Letta

TO START WITH

DESIGN FOR YOU was chosen as our title because it emphasizes the various ways in which we may study, see, produce, or appreciate organizations of lines, shapes, spaces, colors, and textures as they are created for use in our everyday lives. The designs may represent the plan of a building, a drawing of a bowl to be turned on a lathe, a sketch of a design to be scratched in clay and sand for a wallpiece, or the design for a piece of jewelry, a dress, a bag, a mural, or a piece of sculpture. There is no limit.

The ideas throughout this book are the outgrowth of work with students in classes in Freshman Design. Our contacts have been mainly with students who have come to college with little or no previous art training. They may not understand the goals of the artist and his philosophy or the techniques he uses. We do feel, however, that most individuals have an appreciation for beauty and a sense of order. It is a source of gratification for students to realize that they are also capable of creating their own designs.

It is our hope that the information in these chapters will be of value to anyone interested in developing an appreciation of art. We hope that teachers will find this book helpful in developing in their students a working knowledge of basic factors in the organization and evaluation of designs of their own and those of the past. We also hope that the book will be a definite aid to those interested in the expression of originality.

Heretofore, some instructors have made many attempts to introduce the art student to the meaning of design by concentrating on the "principles of design." Others have cast aside all this disciplined study and have used an experimental approach, hoping that the student would absorb a working knowledge of how to create and evaluate his designs by working with materials in a more or less trial-and-error method. Although few have enough imagination or attain great technical ability to become artists of note, we feel nevertheless that everyone can attain some appreciation that encompasses both intellectual understanding and emotional response to his own designs as well as to those created by ones more talented than he. We also feel that a certain amount of rational or disciplined study as suggested in these chapters will help the student to achieve a sensitivity to ways of applying the principles of design with a certain amount of skill.

In our civilization it is necessary for us to be able to read and write even if we are not authors. Similarly it should be necessary for the student of art to acquire a vocabulary of terms pertaining to his creative experiences that he can understand and use. This knowledge should in no way hinder his creative thinking. On the contrary, it should stimulate it and enable him to have more logical reasons for his original experiments.

Thus we have tried in the following chapters to:

(1) combine this basic knowledge of art terms both in vocabulary and in background for evaluation, and

(2) give suggestions for creative experiences, and

(3) help the student appreciate the important place that art occupies in our everyday lives.

The discussions of art terms and the experiments are concentrated on the visual arts only. The suggested experiments are planned to go from the more simple two-dimensional to the more complex three-dimensional ones.

The information concerning the principles of design has been grouped in one chapter, whereas each element of design is given a separate chapter. Although this arrangement may imply that we feel the elements are more important, this is not our purpose. We feel, however, that the approach to creative design can be motivated more successfully by concentrating on the elements. The principles become, then, important guides for evaluating their organization.

No statement or exercise should be interpreted as a formula or pattern to be followed in toto. The teacher or student may find the exercises at the ends of each chapter a way of leading him into free experimentation so that he becomes more conscious of his own resources. We hope that each will use his own imagination to adapt these exercises to his particular needs, tools, materials, and techniques.

We wish to thank Design Today, Inc. for their generosity in allowing us to photograph many contemporary items in their shop.

Our special thanks go to our co-workers and students in the Department of Art for their many helpful suggestions and for their constant loyal support in this work.

ETHEL JANE BEITLER
BILL LOCKHART

March, 1969

CONTENTS

LIST OF ILLUSTRATIONS

CHAPTER 2, GUIDEPOSTS FOR ORGANIZATION

CHAPTER 3, WHAT'S YOUR LINE?

CHAPTER 4, THE SHAPE OF THINGS

CHAPTER 5, SPACE, ALL OR NOTHING

CHAPTER 6, COLOR SOUNDS OFF

CHAPTER 9, DESIGN SPEAKS OUT

CHAPTER 10, THE END AND THE BEGINNING

DESIGN FOR YOU

DESIGN FOR OUR AGE

Since the beginning of time individuals, groups, and whole nations have been concerned with countless design problems dealing with the planning of their homes, their furnishings, their wearing apparel, and their communities. These problems involved design for the particular age in which these people lived, so they might have more personal satisfaction both in the use of items concerned and also in their visual appeal.

Throughout history the taste of designers has constantly altered. Many factors that may cause these changes are (1) the designer's educational background; (2) the available materials, tools, machines, and other equipment that might be utilized by the designer; (3) the purpose for which he plans his design; and (4) his ability to cope with the changes in civilization over a period of time. All of these, and many more, are sufficient causes for the constant succession of designs. The variations become obvious when we compare the Wright brothers' first airplane to present-day jet airliners or space rockets. Each improvement in air power necessitated alterations in basic design. The autogyro, which was flown in the 1930's, was the first attempt to develop an airplane that was capable of vertical flight. The autogyro was a conventional type of airplane, with minor modification, and with a large rotary blade mounted on top of the plane. This plane was flown with some success, but made little contribution to air transportation. During the early 1940's, however, the helicopter

Fig. 1-1 Ward A. Neff Memorial Fountain, located at the University of Missouri, suggests informal balance. It is a combination of sand casting, epoxy resin, and cast stone. It symbolizes "Freedom of the Press . . . Light of the World." (Made by Joseph Falsetti, Associate Professor of Home Economics, University of Missouri.)

made a major contribution to air transportation. Probably the difference in the success of these two similar aircraft was in the design, for the helicopter was not dependent upon modification of the original airplane. The designers of the helicopter had to modify their concept of what an aircraft should look like.

PROGRESS

There is no progress without change, but change is not necessarily progress. It is highly desirable that these changes be beneficial to mankind. Our main problem is to be able to discriminate between that which should be discarded and that which should be kept, built upon, and improved.

Some changes are made just to be different. Some are a gradual outgrowth of past experiences that cause us to alter designs for more valid reasons. For instance, we have used fireplaces in our homes since homes were first built. Today, however, with mechanical heating systems, the fireplace is not necessary for heating purposes, but is used more for an effect of hospitality and the aesthetic quality achieved from the warm glow and the interesting crackle and movement of the flames. However, fireplaces of stone and brick are relatively expensive to build. A "FireHOOD," as illustrated in Fig. 1-2, provides the above-mentioned qualities and is less expensive to install. Critical thinking will enable us to make wise decisions in a world where rapidly changing styles, quick turnover, and built-in obsolescence are common phrases in the industrial and merchandising worlds.

Alexander Girard says, "Designs that are fresh, interesting, and different are not achieved if to be fresh, interesting, and different is the prime objective."

We must stress that the mechanical act of seeing in itself is not awareness. Awareness results in conscious perceiving. This perceiving not only includes seeing and feeling but also registering the response from your total being.

With the dawning of this awareness, understanding can develop. This understanding involves making critical judgments. In relationship of under-

Fig. 1-2 The FireHOOD represents a new concept of design for warmth and beauty in a contemporary home. (Courtesy of Condon-King Co., Inc.)

standing to design we need to develop a sensitivity to design elements. For the beginning student the guides or principles of design may be used to evaluate the organization of the elements. It is our hope that this organization of the elements leads to a more pleasing design. The time and place a design is produced should be considered when we make design judgments. Therefore there should also be understanding and sympathy with the variance of ideas expressed in designs of other present-day cultures. For example, on the San Blas Islands off the coast of Panama the native women and children do not have their ears pierced as many do in our own country; they pierce the nose so a ring can be dangled from it—their idea of beauty. They do not pencil the eyebrows as young women do in our own culture; they place a line vertically along the center of the nose. Their beads are wrapped around their arms instead of their necks. It isn't our place to ridicule or laugh at such practices, but to try to be aware of the underlying reasons behind the differences between their customs and our own. Esther Warner in her "Art An Everyday Experience" states, "there are as many paths to beauty as there are to God." Different people should struggle to attain what they *believe* to be beautiful, not necessarily accept what others say is beautiful. Awareness of beauty requires deep perception. Unless one can appreciate the beauty of a lowly weed he cannot appreciate the beauty of a cultivated plant. Too often the individual is conditioned by taste, income, or social strata. He must find a medium ground of educated response to true beauty, rather than the adult dependence on human opinion or the child's joyous and spontaneous reactions without question.

DESIGN

In all fields of endeavor one needs a working vocabulary related to that particular area of activity to be able to communicate and exchange ideas with others. In the field of art, the term *design* can be interpreted broadly in a number of ways.

1. *Design* may be a noun referring to a particular *organization of elements* for a special object of art. In Chapter 4 on "The Shape of Things" will be a further discussion of the requirements of satisfactory structural and decorative designs. Thus we see that a structural design may be the contour or organization of parts of the object itself, such as a building, a chair, or a vase. Or the *design* may be a decorative pattern that results from the way in which the bricks are organized for the wall construction of the building, or the allover pattern woven into the upholstery fabric for the chair, or the design scratched by the potter into the moist clay.

A design may suit a utilitarian purpose but be sadly lacking in qualities that might give it beauty, or vice versa. The spout of a coffee pot may be excellent for pouring but difficult to clean. The lines of the coffee pot

Fig. 1-3 Present-day machine-made furniture makes no attempt to copy the designs of the past. Metal framework used with wood for drawers and shelves, cabinets with hard plastic tops, and adjustable arrangements harmonize with our contemporary scheme of living. (Comprehensive Storage System designed by George Nelson for the Herman Miller Furniture Company.)

may give it a quality of stateliness and grace, yet it may be very inconvenient because the top keeps falling off when it is tilted for pouring.

2. *Design* may be a verb referring to the *act of designing;* selecting and arranging of those selections for a particular purpose. As with the noun, the purpose may be a *utilitarian* one, such as planning the height of a lamp and the width of the shade to give a wide enough spread of light for use in reading. It may be the selection of component parts assembled in a wall storage system as that shown in Fig. 1-3. The individual finds that he needs open shelves for books, vertical dividers for

7

portfolios, drawers for some items that need to be stored out of sight, and a flip-down desk area for occasional writing purposes.

The purpose may be an *aesthetic* one, such as planning the height of a lamp and the width of the shade to give a sense of pleasing proportions in relation to the table on which the lamp is placed, and the chair beside it. Or it may be the arrangement of open and closed storage space, the size and division of space in drawer units for aesthetic beauty in the comprehensive storage system, as illustrated in Fig. 1-3.

Each design is a definite act which should represent creative thinking. Whether we are *designing* or creating a *design,* we assemble *lines, shapes* or *forms, textures,* and *colors* in a *space.* These, then, are referred to as the *elements of design.* In a broad sense, they are the tools and materials with which everyone makes a design. Over the past century or more our attitude toward "design" has gradually changed. Formerly it was more frequently thought of in relation to an applied decoration or pattern, such as wallpaper or printed fabric. Today we refer more to the *act of designing* which encompasses all our acts of selection and arrangement. Those may include the problem of selecting lines and colors for a design on the drawing board, or selecting lines and colors for the furnishings of a room. Thus design is a problem for everyone, not just for students with so-called artistic ability. Consequently, each of us needs a thorough background in an appreciation of the *elements of design,* how to create with them, and how to evaluate their arrangement according to the *principles of balance, proportion, emphasis,* and *rhythm.* In the following chapters we shall strive to provide that background.

APPROACHES TO DESIGN

The purpose of this book is not to set up rules of organization for the elements of design, but rather to help the student of design to develop a philosophy or creative approach to design—"a way of life." This awareness should enable him to appreciate the works of other artists in his own and earlier periods.

Fig. 1-4 The linear design of the church might have been inspired by an historical cathedral. (Student design.)

HISTORICAL APPROACH

The historical approach to design is not stressed in this book, but the serious student can gain inspiration from awareness of characteristic historical details, philosophy of expression, and ways of living in previous generations. Philip C. Beam in his "The Language of Art" has an excellent discussion of the history of art which is divided into five parts: art of the Western and Eastern hemispheres, art of the various regions, nationalities, periods, and expression of individuality. Great awareness of the past serves in two ways to help promote design sensitivity. First, understanding how the designer is influenced by his time will serve to show the multiple influences that affect present-day designs. Second, sources for today's design are readily available from design from the past. A renaissance cathedral might have been the inspiration for the simple line design in the contemporary manner shown in Fig. 1-4.

ENVIRONMENTAL APPROACH

A designer may gain inspiration from the study of birds (ornithology), of fish (ichthyology), of animals (biology and zoology), of plant life (botany), of the human figure (anatomy), of the earth's structure (geology), and many more areas of science in our universe.

Scientists have found rare beauty in common rocks. Many rocks appear dull and uninteresting to the average viewer, but when viewed under special microscopes that polarize light, thin slices of rocks appear as beautiful abstract paintings.

A study of vast oceans show greater mountain ranges, longer plains, deeper gorges and valleys, than any found on the continents. Forces that unite the oceans and keep them in constant motion, such as wind, rotation of the earth's surface, and the changing density of the water produce restless waves which in turn give rhythmical patterns to excite the imagination of the designer. Constant changes in the appearance of the mountains and plains of the land areas, however, are so slow they are scarcely noticeable. And yet, over the centuries earthquakes change the design of the land, storms grind away the rocks, winds blow the soil and the sand to new areas. There are never two places on the earth that are just alike. Every inch of the earth's surface, under the sea, and the canopy of the air provides ideas for designs for those who will look for them.

Fantastic creatures of the earliest known periods of animal, bird, and fish life provide one with ideas more strange and fascinating than those that an artist could create from his own imagination in present-day surroundings. Plant life throughout the world, on land and in the water, provide limitless ideas to the observing designer. How many plants do you recognize by the design of their leaves? How can you simplify their shapes, adapt them to the purpose of your own design, and give them your own personal charm? See Fig. 1-5. Note the illustrations shown in Figs. 1-6a and b and 1-7. The wallpiece inspired by the rock with the hole in it, the wallpiece created by observing the rise of bubbles and foam in a stein of beer (see Fig. 6-15), the abstract yarn and tissue paper collage developed from a diagram of a heart in an anatomy text are all examples

Fig. 1-5 Rhythmical linear sketch of a plant form inspired from nature. (Student design, Robert A. Wiggs, Faculty, University of South Western Louisiana.)

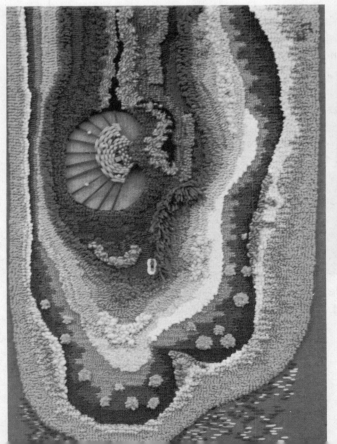

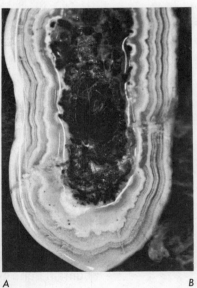

A   B

Fig. 1-6 A, hooked wallpiece inspired from the linear pattern in the slice of rock shown in B. (Designer, Ethel Jane Beitler; owner, Dr. Grover E. Murray.)

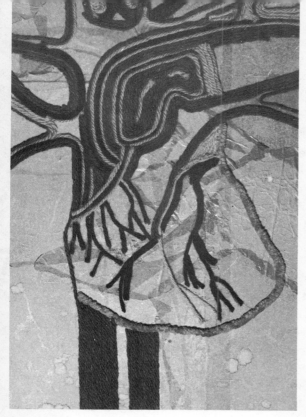

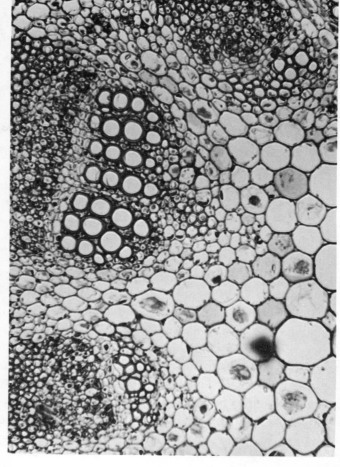

of ideas from nature. Can you visualize the many ways you might gain inspiration from the photomicrograph shown in Fig. 1-8 of the transverse section of a sunflower stem? It might develop into an idea for a pebble mosaic, a hooked rug, a fabric design, or dozens of other creative projects.

Besides all these millions of forms from our natural environment, add to these the products of man-made environment—rolls of wire, rows of tile, structures of buildings, nuts, bolts, and gears, all have their own power of attraction and interesting stimulation for the one who will learn to "see" with his heart as well as his eyes. See Figs. 1-9 through 1-11 for examples of man-made products that might serve as inspiration for abstract or non-objective designs.

11

EXPERIMENTAL APPROACH

Besides this awareness of the value of a thorough study of history and environment, we must not forget the importance of uninhibited experimentation with materials, tools, and processes. Using a brush and paint, for instance, can lead us into many variations of designs with just lines. We may paint with only the tip of the brush. We may load the brush with paint and paint with a shaky hand motion to produce a jagged line effect. We may create a dry-brush effect by using less paint in the brush. We may paint on a damp surface so the lines run together, blending the colors in the process.

This exploring of a material, even though it is one with which the student is familiar, may lead to many new and exciting discoveries of its personality and character. It becomes increasingly important for the designer to constantly reexamine processes and the materials that he uses. For example, most people think that they are familiar with paper, yet how many have examined the numerous ways in which paper is used in today's society? Everyone has folded paper, but few people have seen the delightful curves that may be folded in a piece of paper. Paper—one of the flimsier materials—may be folded and creased so that it gains the strength to stand by itself. In fact, not only may it stand, but two sheets of construction paper, weighing a fraction of an ounce, are capable of

Fig. 1-9 The curved lines of the steel rod structure are a reinforcement for concrete columns used as a building foundation. The hazy lines are reflections in water puddles. The combination of lines might offer inspiration for an interesting line pattern. (Photograph by Don Murray.)

Fig. 1-10 Geometric arrangement of concrete blocks could offer inspiration for a pleasing pattern.

Fig. 1-11 Linear pattern made by rolls of wire.

supporting fifteen or twenty pounds of weight. Thus, the student who sees new possibilities in the use of paper will be in a good position to apply new and exciting designs to paper. Refer to the paper sculptured design in Fig. 1-12. Can you see how this might lead to an interesting model for metal sculpture as well as giving joy to the designer in working with colorful pieces of paper?

Actually, the more you know about a material, and about the tools and equipment for working with it, the more difficult it is to experiment to arrive at still different ways of working. In the early stages of the industrial revolution in the mid-nineteenth century the craftsman in wood, freed from the necessity of using hand tools and time-consuming labor, became carried away with what power tools could do. The work of this time became overdecorated with applied forms that had been mechanically produced to represent hand carving. This can still be seen in the "gingerbread" trim on Victorian homes.

The experimentation is not insurance of good design. But as the designer becomes better acquainted with his materials, tools, and equipment he is better able to have aesthetically pleasing results. Note the design of the eagle in Fig. 1-13. The craftsman has experimented with his carving tools sufficiently so he is skilled enough to be able to cut paper-thin sheets of wood that curl upward to form the decorative wings

13

and tail feathers and has applied this skill satisfactorily for an exciting result.

All designs should grow out of the material of which it is made. We may gain inspiration from the designs of others. However, our creativeness will be reflected in the degree of our individual interpretation. The design might be based on age-old forms, most of which are found in nature, but we should attempt to discover a new approach. A design that is planned in a very unusual manner just for the sake of uniqueness will no doubt lack true beauty and depth of character.

INDIVIDUAL APPROACH

Under the experimental approach stress has been placed on experimenting and examining our materials, but we must also examine the ways and methods in which we as individuals work best. As in the case of materials, each person has his strengths and limitations. It has been said that our success depends on our ability to play up our strengths and play down our weaknesses. The only problem with this is that we often make mistakes as to what our strengths are. A student will say how weak he is in three-dimensional work, then find himself confronted with a problem that must be met in three-dimensions, and suddenly become involved and find he had sold himself short.

There are as many different ways of working as there are individuals. One may find an interesting piece of wood that suggests to him the shape of a giraffe. He may carve and shape to strengthen his idea and finish with a piece of wood sculpture depicting a giraffe. Another person may say, "I'm going to make a giraffe," and proceed to look for an appropriate piece of wood that could be used for that purpose. By either method, the end result would be similar. One starts with the material and lets it suggest to him what he can do with it. This method may be considered a more spontaneous approach. The other has a definite idea in mind before he selects the material and then chooses it and works with it accordingly. This would be considered a more deliberate approach. Actually most of us will use a combination of these approaches and this book will not defend one method as being better. The deliberate approach will

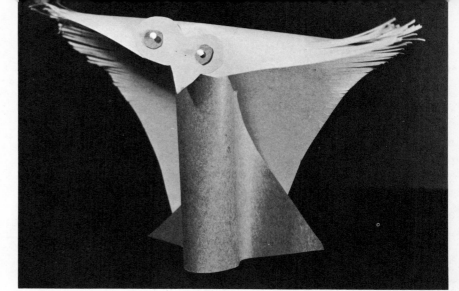

Fig. 1-12 Using a natural form for inspiration, a student may create an abstract form that has personality and intriguing details.

Fig. 1-13 Skillful manipulation of carving tools produced the rhythmical suggestion of feathers on the wings and tail on the wooden eagle. (Photograph courtesy of Design Today, Inc.)

have problems when a lack of knowledge of the materials and processes may cause the student to attempt to force his material into a desired shape. This student would do well to either use a more spontaneous approach or to experiment with his materials sufficiently until he knows better how to select his materials and work with them to create the desired design. No matter how well he knows himself and his way of working it is important to explore and know the materials available to him. As the designer becomes better acquainted with himself, his materials and processes, his work will evidence more unity between the design and materials used.

We must each work in a way best suited to our temperaments and individual abilities. This may seem a very simple statement, but *our* success as an individual designer depends not only on understanding this statement, but on our ability to put this into practice!

In each of the chapters dealing with the elements of design there will be suggestions for studio problems using the four above-mentioned "approaches to design." Let them guide you along your pathway to creative design. You should never lack sources for inspiration. The main problem should be in making a selection from the wide number of sources available for you to use.

PURPOSE OF THE DESIGN

Design today, as always, is directed by the combination of tools and materials, methods of construction, and purpose or use of the design. The familiar statement that "form follows function" may not be as clear to some as the statement that "function should determine form and form should express function." But tradition may hamper us in spite of our best intentions. For generations, we have associated the design of a table knife with that of a long, narrow blade. A designer may be ridiculed when he insists that the blade can just as well be short and broad to give one the ample length for cutting purposes and the width necessary for spreading butter. We may have been accustomed to the long, thin tines on a table fork on which it is difficult to balance peas. Yet we may be reluctant to accept a new design of a fork with short, broad tines and a curved bowl

Fig. 1-14 The variation of the thickness and the contour of the vase lends a simple dignity to the shape. The lack of ornamentation also emphasizes the pleasing use of glass as a material. (Orefors crystal, courtesy Zacho, Inc.)

Fig. 1-16 "Focus" pattern in stainless steel, chosen one of the 100 best designs of our time, utilizes the design of the short blade on the knife. (Designed by Folke Arstrom for Gense, Import, Ltd.)

Fig. 1-15 The sculptural beauty of the hand-wrought sterling has a flowing quality of dignified beauty. Note the curved "spoonlike" quality of the forks. ("Tjorn" pattern designed by Jens H. Quistgaard for Dansk Designs, Inc., Great Neck, New York.)

to keep the peas from falling off. The creator of this new knife and fork is only trying to design forms that are determined by the uses that are made of them in cutting, spreading, and transferring food from the plate to the mouth. When we say that "form expresses function," we sense a desire on our part to really use this knife to cut or to spread butter.

Note the tableware shown in Fig. 1-15 and 1-16. The forks are designed so the sides are curved upward slightly. More space is left between the short tines. The short blade on the knife can be used for cutting or spreading. A separate butter spreader is not needed. Both designs of tableware—one in hand-wrought sterling silver, and the one in stainless steel—have simple elegance that gives them lasting beauty.

SUITABLE USES OF MATERIALS

Our designs are what they are because of the materials used in them. Every material, whether it is wood, metal, glass, or plastic, has qualities

17

that make it suitable for particular uses. When we emphasize that fact and do not let tradition interfere and tempt us to make a metal chair frame look like a wooden one, we shall have greater variety of designs that are more beautiful and practical.

In the furnishing of our homes, it seemed inevitable that our early machine-made furniture should try to imitate the work of the skilled cabinetmaker and carver. As machine production grew into mass production, the need to simplify operations and reduce costs produced two results. One was the elimination of the extra details, and the other was the loss of individual craftsmanship. Gradually there emerged the realization that wood itself is beautiful in its exposed, undecorated state. It is available in a great variety of forms and quantities. It lends itself to a multitude of techniques with which it can be turned into objects of beauty.

Then in the last century along came the designer who conceived the idea that furniture could be made of metal. Unfortunately, tradition stunted his imagination. Like his ancestors who had tried to imitate the skilled carvers in their machine-made designs, he imitated the designs in wood (see Fig. 1-17). The metal products were even painted and

Fig. 1-17 Trite attempt to imitate natural plant forms in metal. Uncomfortable back, exaggerated decoration on legs.

grained to simulate the exact appearance of wood. Fairly recently we have realized that we can design beautiful furniture that is frankly made of metal, undisguised, and in new forms suited to the natural material of metal rather than of wood. We know that such furniture can have sparkle, grace, charm, comfort, and durability. We know, also, that if we want the other virtues of warmth, richness, and traditional beauty we can turn to wood, proving that we can plan a design that best suits the material.

We can go further in our discussion of the knife and fork and compare the early designs in stainless steel tableware with traditional ones in silver. The idea was prevalent in the minds of housewives that silver was the only beautiful material for flatware. Therefore, when stainless steel designers attempted to get their ideas accepted, they imitated the earlier patterns in silver, making it look cheap and penny-saving. When designers and consumers were willing to open their eyes to the beauty of stainless steel as a material, the designers could then begin to create the simple, unadorned, and sculptured forms that the housewife had to admit she had admired all along but was afraid to select in silver because it was easily scratched and marred.

EXPRESSION OF GOOD TASTE

It is no less important for those of us who are consumers to have a knowledge of art quality than it is for us who are merchants with the responsibility of stocking our shelves with items for others to buy. The merchant is naturally interested in the money value of an object, but in most cases that object will have greater sale value if it is well designed.

On the other side of the picture, it is evident that the ability to recognize good art quality is not always sufficient. Many times there are limitations to the expression of good taste.

1. The likes and dislikes of people who are going to use the items.
2. The availability of items limited because of certain economic or political upheavals or shortage of materials.
3. The number or kind of items one has on hand.
4. The prevailing fashions.

19

All the above might cause us to alter our choices, regardless of our store of knowledge of basic principles of design. If we can learn to make wise choices, considering both utility and beauty, and learn to live with our selections and be just plain happier, then art has found a definite place in our daily lives.

What is the role of the student in developing skills and understanding of design? No text or course by itself can guarantee that a student will develop the knowledge and understanding of design. There must be a willingness and an interest. He must study, see, feel, and evaluate his reactions. The student must explore and experiment. To gain a knowledge of design, he must be willing to examine his prejudices and be flexible. No written material will explain design unless the student makes an effort to examine what is presented. Many points may seem strange and even shocking. What if traditional church architecture as built today is criticized as being poor taste? Are you as a student willing to examine this statement? Could there be truth in such shocking words? Many times your emotional attachments may make you intolerant. Deep personal involvement with religion and warm feelings for the place of worship make it hard to accept criticism of a place of worship. If you tell someone that his church is poorly designed, his first reaction is apt to be negative. He may feel that you are criticizing his church, his religion, and even himself. To become a real student of design, you must be willing to examine your surroundings critically, even though many of these objects may be important for sentimental reasons. You must attempt to be as objective as possible, although it is doubtful that any person can become completely objective. You must recognize that our emotional make-up will have much to do with the light in which we view design. See Fig. 1-18 for examples of new lines in architecture.

Whether your interest in design will be from the consumer's or producer's point of view, this is the beginning. Girard says, "The hope for good design lies in those designers who believe in what they do and who will only do what they believe. . . ." We further believe that the same is true for the consumer. Are our selections made by what the Jones' have, or what is popular, or do we have the nerve to select what is the best design for us? The authors feel that with increased understanding of

Fig. 1-18 Architects are introducing new lines with both old and new materials into our building designs today. Here the pattern of windows and balconies in the office building provide an exciting conversation piece for the viewer. (United Founders Life Tower, Oklahoma City. Photograph by Don Murray.)

design you not only create a more functional environment but you can also develop a more satisfying environment for your spirit.

When asked what went into a good design, a designer said, "It takes the eye, the hand, the brain, and the heart!" Does it not follow that understanding of good design will also affect these same separate parts in an integrated pattern?

One of the last things that the late Walter Dorwin Teague wrote seems to sum up so well his design philosophy.

Design is like a river that flows slowly. It makes no abrupt changes of direction but over the years its character gradually varies. It carries on its current many beautiful things out of the past which we still treasure even though we have no desire to copy them today. We should hope that the things we do now will have similar values for the future.

2

GUIDEPOSTS FOR ORGANIZATION

Fig. 2-1 Organization of lines, forms, textures, and space. (Church of Religious Science in Los Angeles. Photograph by Don Murray.)

TASTE REFLECTS KNOWLEDGE

Our taste is reflected in the things we select. Our training, understanding, and experiences, as well as our intuitive sense, are responsible for molding our tastes. If we are flexible in our attitudes and have acquired a treasure house of knowledge that should aid us in making our selections, then we are never forced to make a poor choice through lack of knowledge. By learning to make our training and experiences work for us, we can learn to get the most out of our *faculties*. It is said that there are none so blind as those who will not see. It is not expected that everyone with the same training and experience will make the same selections. There are always personal reasons for likes and dislikes that may alter one's choices, but the fact remains that the person who will not make use of his training to aid him in making wiser choices and who chooses items only because he likes them, with no logical reasons to explain his selections, may soon find himself set in his ways and inclined to be narrow minded in his tastes.

All our acts of selection and arrangement are decisions in design. Whether it is in the painting of a picture, the carving of a piece of wood sculpture, the planting of a garden, or in the selection and arrangement of furnishings for a room, we are making a design decision. This decision involves our likes and dislikes, our human needs, and the application of the guideposts for organization or the *principles of design:* balance, proportion, emphasis, and rhythm. See Fig. 2-1.

FACTORS IN CREATING A DESIGN

All of us work (1) *in a variety of ways* when we create designs. No two people will approach a problem in exactly the same manner. This *creative factor* sets one design apart from another and gives it life and meaning. This factor is difficult to analyze and logically explain. It may be favored or disfavored by circumstances. All of us have (2) *different needs* that will alter our choices. Those needs may be economic, physical, psychological, or emotional. (3) The *materials* that are available at the time we are planning the design will most assuredly influence our choices. At no time in history has the designer had such a profusion of materials with which to work as he has today. This fact alone might actually make the designer's task more difficult because of the vast store of knowledge he needs concerning the possibilities and limitations of all these materials. However, this wide variety of materials might make the designer's taste more exciting and challenging. (4) We are influenced by the *locality* where the design is created and used. This is especially obvious in home architecture; warmer climates influence the architectural design. (5) The *tools and processes* which we use in the development of the design will alter our individual approach to the problem. When we group all these factors with the application of principles of design and allow for changes resulting from our many likes and dislikes, it is no wonder that there is no end to our changing designs.

ORDER IN DESIGN

All the above factors show a need for basic aims of organization that can be applied in any area of design. First, we must strive for a *sense of order*—of unity—of oneness. This order can be of a regimental type—a planned example of regularity that still satisfies us because of the pleasing way in which the proportions of the various parts of the repeat have been organized. For an allover pattern for wallpaper, gift-wrapping papers, printed fabric design, or floor covering one might find it to his advantage to plan a regimented type of pattern. This mechanical repeat is due largely to the function of the process of printing continuous surfaces. This order can be of a nonregimented type. It should be spontaneous, free, a planned form of irregularity that intrigues the eye, amuses us, satisfies us, or just plain delights us with a feeling of rightness. But whether we plan a regular or an irregular pattern to achieve order, we need to know how to apply the principles of design—proportion, balance, emphasis, and rhythm—guides in using the plastic elements of lines, shapes, colors, textures, and space that compose our design. (For examples of regular and irregular repeats, see photographs in Figs. 2-2, 2-3, 2-4, and 2-5.) Other examples may be found in Chapter 4 in the section on allover patterns.

Order implies a feeling of unity or a sense of structure, but we need to go further than just a trite application of principles of design and arrive at a *sense of beauty* achieved through a knowledge of when to vary that orderly arrangement. To know when and where to introduce *variety* in unity necessitates constant observation, study, experimentation, and practice to arrive at the point where we can say that we can create a good design. (See Figs. 2-1, 2-2, 2-3, 2-4, and 2-5.)

PROPORTION

Proportion is the principle of design that involves a pleasing relationship between all parts of the design in relation to each other and to the whole.

1. This principle may include the planning of the *basic shapes* within a design. Shall we use a geometric, free-form, abstract, or naturalistic shape? Besides the aesthetic approach, do we need to consider physical contact, such as the shape of a handle to fit the hand or the contour of a chair to fit the body?

2. It may involve the *scale* of the forms within the design. Shall we use

(*upper left*)
Fig. 2-2 Regular repeats that satisfy because of the roughness of the stone that supplies the variety. (Yucatan Stone from Murals, Inc.)

(*upper right*)
Fig. 2-3 Irregularity of sizes of the same shape provide variety with unity. (Yucatan Stone from Murals, Inc.)

(*lower left*)
Fig. 2-4 Regular repeats of circles which satisfy because of the irregular variation of values of dark and light. (''Circles,'' designed by Alexander Girard for Herman Miller Furniture Company.)

(*lower right*)
Fig. 2-5 Irregularity of sizes of the same shape again provides variety with unity. (''One-Way,'' designed by Alexander Girard for the Herman Miller Furniture Company.)

large forms, small ones, medium ones, or a combination of these?

3. How shall we *divide the space* for the overall design and each of its parts and/or group the various sizes together? How can we achieve beautiful space relationships where variety of shape, size, and the general unity of idea are to be expressed?

4. How can we *create satisfying optical illusions* that will give the impression of beautiful proportions when it is not possible or feasible to change the basic design?

26

Fig. 2-6 Glassware assumes a quality of formality or informality because of its length of stem or weight. "Tango" pattern in Royal Leerdam is more informal because of the short stems on the iced tea and sherbet. This set was awarded the hallmark of "Good Design" of the New York Museum of Modern Art. Designed by A. D. Copier. (Photograph courtesy of A. J. Van Dugteren and Sons, Inc.)

PLANNING THE BASIC SHAPE

In Chapter 4 on shape and form there is a more extensive discussion of these elements from the standpoint of their selection and use in a design. At this point, we are mainly interested in the way in which the element of shape is involved with the principle of proportion. With each of the principles of design there are no rigid laws that can or should be applied in the development of a design. There are suggestions, however, which might aid the student or amateur artist in *developing a sensitivity* for good design.

In creating beautiful proportions, one suggestion might be inspired from the statement of John Dewey: "There is no excellent beauty that hath not some strangeness in the proportion." This does not mean, of course, that every object which is unusual in form, fantastic, exotic, or grotesque is beautiful in proportion. "Strangeness" in this sense would mean that one refrains from too much repetition and knows when to introduce just enough variety to add interest. That variety may be in the tumbler which is tapered at the bottom to keep the proportions of the sides from expressing too much sameness. It may also be tapered to make it more convenient to grasp in the hand or it may be larger at the top to make it easier to clean. Note the glassware shown in, Figs. 2-6, 2-7, and 2-8. Each piece is planned from the standpoint of function and

(far left)
Fig. 2-7 "Patrician" pattern in Lobmeyr crystal is delicate, fragile in appearance, and very formal in character because of its tall, thin stem. (Executed by J. and L. Lobmeyr, Vienna, Austria. Designed by Professor Joseph Hoffman of the Vienna Academy of Applied Arts, 1918.)

(near left)
Fig. 2-8 "Princess" pattern in Danish crystal is heavy, because of its thick base, and presents a more informal air. (Photograph courtesy of Gematex, Inc.)

aesthetic beauty. In Fig. 2-6 the short stems make the glassware seem more informal for daily family use. It won't be so easily broken as the long, slender stem on the goblet shown in Fig. 2-7. The tall goblet, however, is very stately and beautiful for a formal occasion. Most families could plan to handle the slender stems more carefully for those few occasions when they entertain more formally. The goblet in Fig. 2-8 has an unusual base of solid glass to give necessary weight at the bottom, so the goblet will stand more firmly without a stem or thin flat base as shown in the other pieces of glassware. The structural design shows unity with variety in the shape of the upper part of the goblet in relation to the base. The decorative design consists of just a small air bubble in the shape of a tear drop in the base. This lends interest and character to an already beautiful structural shape. Each piece of glassware shown is functionally acceptable for drinking purposes because the sides do not curve inward, causing one to dribble.

In general, shapes that are just as wide as they are tall may not be

Fig. 2-9 A and B Although the proportions were determined by the suggested contents of the package, the decorative designs show a sensitive relationship to the structural form. (Class project designed by Jerry Stevens, student in Architecture and Allied Arts Department, Texas Tech University.)

as pleasing as those that vary in their horizontal and vertical measurements. The purpose for which the design is to be used and the processes to be followed in the completion of the project may determine to a great extent the ways in which we may successfully apply the principle of proportion. The design of a cardboard carton to be used in marketing a product might need to have straight sides so that the cartons can be stacked next to each other and on top of one another. The height, width, and depth of the carton would need to be planned in proportions that would enclose most satisfactorily the product to be marketed, and that could be made most economically from available cardboard stock. This carton might possibly develop into one that was cubical in shape, having the same rather monotonous vertical and horizontal measurements. For a utilitarian object such as this, however, the proportions would more likely be planned to suit the purpose of the design, and the art quality or beauty would be expressed in the accuracy of workmanship and in the easy manipulation in the opening and closing of the carton.

Note the design of the carton for the telephone, as shown in Figs. 2-9a and b. The rectangular shape of the structural design was planned to house the telephone and receiver, and the boxes will easily stack for shipping purposes and for storage of large quantities in the warehouse. The decorative design on the exterior of the box symbolizes the dial on the telephone, and is planned so the design is different on all sides of the box, but is harmonious with the overall design. Both structural and decorative designs were planned specifically for the telephone.

On the other hand, if one were planning the proportions of a box to be used as a jewelry case, there would be no limitations such as the storage and marketing problems mentioned in the design of the cardboard carton. One could plan the jewelry case to be longer than deep, and the height shorter than the depth. The sides could be vertical or sloped, curved or straight; the edge could be sharp or rounded. The main problem would be (1) to plan a pleasing ratio between all measurements to avoid too much sameness or too much variety; (2) to plan a design that was not like every other jewelry box on the market, but that expressed a new quality in design that gave one a satisfied feeling of beauty; and (3) to plan it to meet the function of holding the specific pieces of jewelry for which it was designed. The above three factors can be developed into

29

important generalizations that can be used to evaluate the proportions of other shapes and forms.

SCALE OF OBJECTS

To be completely sensitive to beautiful proportions, one must be familiar with the underlying significance of *scale.* This is the relationship between sizes within an object and those of other objects used with it. Scale involves an understanding of the *principle of ratios.* We may observe that one rectangle is two inches wide and three inches long; it is the ratio of 2:3. Another rectangle is four inches wide and six inches long. It also is the ratio of 2:3; therefore, it is the same proportion as the first rectangle, but it is twice as large in scale. The graphic artist is well aware of this principle when he plans art work for reproduction purposes. He knows that his final design, when reproduced, must be 2″ x 3″. But he wishes to make his inked rendering larger in scale so that any irregularities of line or fuzziness of edges will be less evident when the plate is reduced to the 2″ x 3″ size. He knows, also, that the inked rendering must not only be larger in size but also have the same proportion. Therefore, if a line is drawn diagonally from corner to corner and projected outward, any rectangle that would be formed with this diagonal line bisecting the corner would be the same proportion as the 2″ x 3″ form. (See diagram in Fig. 2-10.)

The interior designer should be especially conscious of scale in selecting furnishings for a room. More will be discussed later in this chapter on the problem of using scale to create optical illusions. At this point we are concerned primarily with the use of scale to create beautiful proportions. A large, bulky piece of furniture is not necessarily comfortable because of its size. Chairs that are small in scale, thin of line, may be especially comfortable due to the use of foam rubber under the upholstery. Several large, bulky pieces of furniture in a small room may appear entirely too large in scale, whereas the same number of pieces in smaller scale might give a very pleasing effect.

In costume design our sense of rightness demands that articles of apparel worn together should not show too great a difference in size

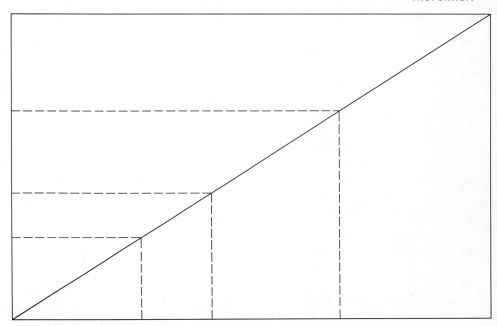

Fig. 2-10 Any square or rectangular shape may be reduced in scale and kept the same shape by dividing diagonally through the center and drawing lines parallel to the sides of the original shape.

relationship to the wearer and to each other. This size relationship might be applied to separate parts of the ensemble, such as the hat, bag, jewelry, fur scarf, or collar—all consistent with the scale of the wearer. It would also apply to the individual parts within the garment, such as the collar, cuffs, pockets, sleeves, trimming details, or surface patterns and textures of fabrics in relation to the size of the wearer and to each other. A dainty young lady would be overburdened with a large picture hat and a purse the size of a shopping bag. Occasionally for dramatic effect, however, one might wish to use an under or oversized, out-of-scale proportion. In an advertisement, an illustration of a chair might occupy a full page.

In choosing sizes of objects for an arrangement, such as a grouping of pictures on a wall, accessories on a table or open shelf, or parts of a centerpiece, a fine sense of proportion and scale must be considered. The ability to select harmony of size without either too much likeness or unlikeness—a pleasing difference—cannot be achieved in a day. Constant observation and experimentation with a variety of sizes leads one to an ever-broadening awareness of beautiful proportions. (See large and small scale designs in Figs. 2-11 and 12.) Also see Fig. 2-13 in which three sizes of birds are grouped together for a pleasing arrangement.

DIVISION OF SPACE

One of the most important problems faced by the designer is that of organizing the total area into fine space relations. Pleasing proportions, mentioned earlier in this chapter, usually have some quality of "strangeness." It may not be too evident that a space is divided in halves, or thirds, or quarters. On the other hand, neither should the divisions be so unusual that they are difficult to understand and appreciate. For example, many "Op Art" compositions make use of two objects or spaces of equal

Fig. 2-11 A small-scale drapery design harmonizes with the more delicate, curved-line furniture. ("Manhattan," designed by Alexander Girard for the Herman Miller Furniture Company.)

Fig. 2-12 A large-scale drapery design harmonizes with simple, straight-line furniture. ("Giant Rectangles," designed by Alexander Girard for the Herman Miller Furniture Company.)

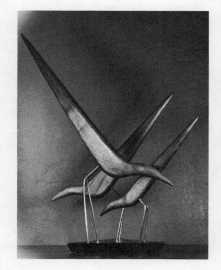

Fig. 2-13 Three sizes of the same shape provide greater possibilities for pleasing arrangements. (Designed by Val Robbins. Photograph courtesy of Jaru Art Products, Inc.)

value, thus creating ambiguity that is as attention holding as it may be boring.

When dividing a space or a line into two parts, as in Fig. 2-14, placing the division close to B would probably be more satisfactory than placing the division exactly at B. Therefore, the space would not be divided exactly in the ratio of 2:3.

Fig. 2-14

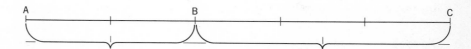

When dividing a space into two parts, the student should avoid dividing the spaces into two equal parts. If both subparts are the same, then interest is lost and there is a danger of boredom. The design must attempt to develop two parts that achieve interest and are still related. (See Fig. 2-15.)

In example (b) although a great amount of contrast has been created between the two shapes, the contrast becomes difficult to handle successfully. Great contrast may be used to produce a dramatic feeling. However, the new student must be careful that this does not become comical or grotesque. Mutt and Jeff are the classic examples of the great contrast in shapes used to create humor. Example (c) illustrates a more interesting division of space.

Fig. 2-15 Usually, spaces that are not divided in the exact center, or too far to the side, show more pleasing division of space.

A   B   C

Division of space into more than two parts might involve repetition of spaces, variation of spaces, or a combination of repetition with variety. The fewer divisions of space, the greater the variety there may be. (See Fig. 2-16.)

Division of space both horizontally and vertically may be done mathematically, planning progressively larger or smaller areas as in the whirling square. Or the eye may be used as a guide in creating a variety of areas that seem to harmonize or contrast with each other in a satisfying manner.

Diagonal lines create a dynamic effect in a composition. One should be careful, however, not to direct one's attention more to a specific corner than to the structural shape. Compare the designs in Fig. 2-17a and b which show diagonal division of space. In (a) the diagonal is right in the center from corner to corner with the circle divided in the middle also. Are not the proportions of (a) more trite and uninteresting than the uneven division in (b)? Study the free-form shape of the ashtray shown in Fig. 2-32. Note the off-center placement of the point at the bottom, with the irregular thickness of the light area surrounding a free-form inner area of dark value. Much more creative thinking is expressed in this design than in a design of a true circle with a border that is the same width all the way around. In Fig. 2-18 a bisymmetrical design is shown, but the variety has been expressed in the fact that the salt shaker flares inward at the exact center and the pepper shaker flares outward. A wider top on the salt shaker also makes it possible to have more and larger holes than are planned for the pepper shaker. This also makes the design more appropriate for the purpose for which it is to be used. In Fig. 2-19 an uneven division of space has been planned with angular shapes. Note

Fig. 2-16 *A, monotonous division of spaces —all the same size. B, Variety of spacing— each one is different. C, Gradation of spacing —small to large. D, Variation of spacing— narrow light spaces, wide dark spaces. E, Variation of spacing—narrow dark spaces, wide light spaces. F, Gradation of spacing—small to large in both light and dark.*

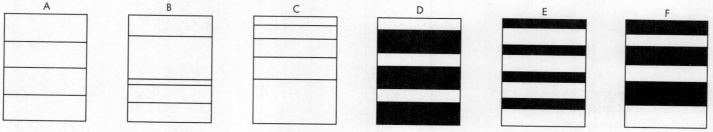

A

B

Fig. 2-17A Space divided diagonally through the center attracts too much attention to the corners and to the equal division of space.

Fig. 2-17B Spaces that are divided off-center stimulate interest and attract more attention to the structural shape.

that the long diagonal does not cut the top and bottom sides at the same distance from the ends. There are large, medium, and small areas developed by the diagonal, horizontal, and vertical divisions of space.

Frequently, in viewing groups of objects, such as pictures on a wall, items on a counter, or repeat-units in a border, we need to consider the amount of space to be left between each object or motif. A good general rule to follow might be: if the objects are to be enjoyed individually, then the space between can be greater than the amount of space occupied by the single unit. If, however, the objects or motifs are to be viewed as a group, then the space between should be less than that occupied by the unit. Consider the stepping stones in a path. If the stones are further apart than the size of the stone so that we have to jump from one stone to the next, we are unable to walk easily along the path. (See Fig. 2-20.)

If objects are overlapped in an arrangement, then a variation in the space overlapped might lend more pleasing relationships in proportion than a "stair-step" arrangement (see Fig. 2-21a and b). In grouping several kinds of shapes together it is usually a good idea to have some similarity of shapes, with perhaps a variety of sizes. In Fig. 2-13 note that the bird shapes are quite similar but are made in three different sizes with the largest one facing in the opposite direction from the other two. This makes a much less regimented design than if they were all lined up in the same direction and in graduated heights.

Fig. 2-18 Although division of space is in the center, the design of the salt and pepper shakers shows variety in the thickness at the center, besides variation of the width of the tops.

CREATING OPTICAL ILLUSIONS

To suggest a change in appearance of an area by means of proportion might involve the lengthening or broadening effects of vertical and horizontal lines. In general, we usually say that lines running in a vertical direction tend to slenderize and make an object appear taller, whereas lines running in a horizontal direction would make an object appear shorter and broader. However, there are exceptions to nearly all "rules." A fabric with narrow to medium stripes used horizontally the full length of a straight sheath-type garment worn by a short, slender figure might tend to create the illusion of height. This illusion is due to the fact that the lines are short horizontally and are extended over a relatively long space from hem to shoulder. If, however, the figure were plump, as well as short, and the stripes were broad, the emphasis would be more on the horizontal direction of the stripes rather than on the illusion of height because of the repetition of the stripes.

You may be familiar with the diagrams where diagonal lines are used to make a line appear shorter or longer. This illusion may be used to advantage in costume design to change the apparent height of a figure by features such as collars, raglan sleeves, necklines, kick pleats, yokes, pockets, seams, or trimming details. See Fig. 2-22.

Scale may play an important role in creating optical illusions. In a small room many large or heavy pieces of furniture, figured upholstery, drapery, wallpaper, or floor covering may reduce the apparent size of the room.

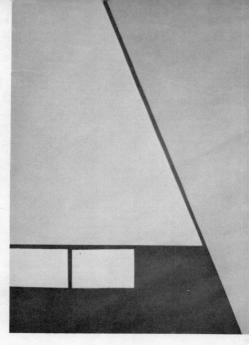

Fig. 2-19 Spaces divided unevenly into large, medium, and small areas creates more pleasing proportions than equal areas. Note the uneven divisions of the top, bottom, and left side—no two of which are the same.

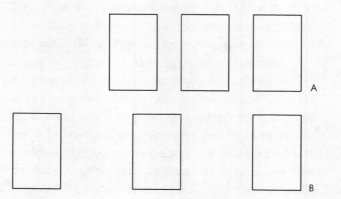

Fig. 2-20 If the units are to be viewed as a group as in A the space between each unit should be less than the width of each unit. If the units are to be viewed individually, then the space should be wider as in B.

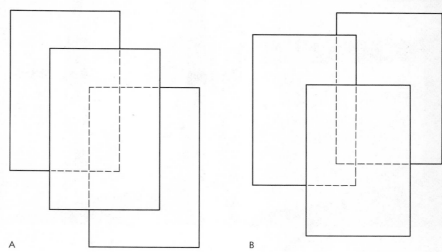

A   B

Fig. 2-21 Monotonous arrangements of shapes as in A may be avoided by overlapping the shapes in an irregular manner as in B.

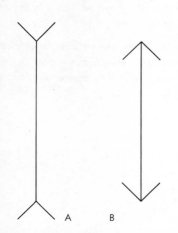

A   B

Fig. 2-22 The vertical lines are the same length, but the diagonal lines in A create the optical illusion of additional length. The diagonal lines in B create the optical illusion of reducing the length.

But place in the same room thin-line furniture, large areas of solid colors, light in value, grayed in intensity with small accents of bright intensities or dark values, and the room may appear much larger. The reverse may be true if we wished to make the room appear smaller. The one exception might be to concentrate more on large areas of low values and grayed intensities rather than on large areas of bright intensities. The large area of bright intensity would reduce the apparent size of the room, but would no doubt be difficult to live with for any length of time because it would be contrary to the "Law of Areas" as discussed later in the chapter on color.

An entire design must be visualized in order to be able to evaluate the principle of proportion correctly. Each part is dependent upon every other part. One part may appear correct when seen by itself but seem entirely out of proportion when seen with other parts of the design. In Fig. 2-23a, b, and c all the white areas are the same size and shape against the black background, but in (a) the horizontal line makes the white area appear wider. In (b) the vertical line makes the space seem taller, while in (c) the vertical line and the small black square are closer to the outer edge and make the white space seem both taller and wider. See Chapter 5 on space for further discussion of creating optical illusions.

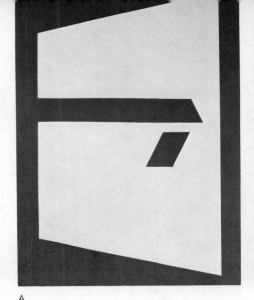

A

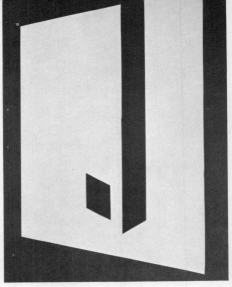

B

C

BALANCE

Balance is the principle of design that gives a feeling of stability due to the illusion of equal tensions or weights on both sides of the composition. Formal or symmetrical balance may be either bisymmetrical or obvious. In other words, same or similar units on each side of the design should be placed equal distances from the center. The fact that the units are the same or similar will indicate that they give the *impression* of equal weights (see Fig. 2-24). Therefore, if they are placed the same distances from the center, they will automatically be balanced. This takes for granted, of course, that the upper and lower portions of the design are so arranged as to give a feeling of balance. Thus there is not the effect of either too much weight at the bottom or a top-heavy appearance. For instance, a dark ceiling may be used to advantage in a room with a high ceiling, but if a low ceiling were made darker in value than the walls it could give one a feeling of claustrophobia. A dark blouse and a light skirt might be worn to advantage by a tall girl, but would make a short person look even shorter.

Formal balance is sometimes referred to as a passive or static balance because of the quiet dignity or stateliness and formality that is evident in its organization. Designs that are stately are sometimes quite active or dynamic in their impressions, however. A steeply sloped roof on a

Fig. 2-23A The horizontal line creates the optical illusion of widening the space in the enclosure.

Fig. 2-23B The vertical line creates the optical illusion of making the space in the enclosure appear taller.

Fig. 2-23C The vertical line placed close to the outer edge creates the optical illusion of making the enclosure appear tall and also wider.

Fig. 2-24 *Almost identical* carving on each side of the wooden sculptured figure relieves the monotony of bisymmetrical formal balance. (Designer, W. J. Westenhaver, Art Director of Witco, Inc.)

church may have an active, moving quality about it that cannot be denied.

The inexperienced person who is not aware of beautiful space variations may not at first succeed in creating a satisfactory example of formal balance, although it is relatively easy to center a picture, a doorway, or a flower arrangement for a centerpiece. One must be sensitive, however, to the ways in which one can employ the principle of formality so that the end result will not be trite and uninteresting.

In planning an informally balanced design, one has many more items to consider: the size and number of shapes or forms grouped on either side of the center; the distance from the center or the distance from the front or back of a design that each form is placed; or the way in which the dark and light, bright or dull, warm and cool forms of colors are used to give a proper feeling of balance.

The diagrams of the scales in Fig. 2-25 may explain the principle of balance, especially in the placement of shapes in a design. In (*a*) the shapes are the same in size, shape, and value of dark and light. They are placed the same distance from the center and thus express formal bisymmetrical balance. In (*b*) the two shapes on the right (when combined) have the same weight as the one on the left. Thus, they also are placed the same distance from the center and give a variation of formal balance which is not so monotonous. In (*c*) the object on the left is much larger than the one on the right, but because it is so light in value, it can be placed the same distance from the center as the dark shape and still give the impression of equal weights on both sides. This also is a variation of formal balance.

In (*d*) the large and small shapes are both dark, showing the impression of heaviness of the larger one so it pulls the scales down on the right. In (*e*), by shifting the smaller shape to the left and bringing the larger shape closer to the center, proper informal balance is achieved.

In these examples we see what happens when "actual weights" are used, whereas in most art problems we are concerned more with creating *optical illusions* of equal weights. A number of different factors may cause a form to *appear* heavier: size, color, texture, decorative pattern, or placement. Automatically, the unit that is made large in size will appear heavier. Actually, it might be constructed of a type of material that would literally make it weigh less than a small object. For instance, a block of balsa wood

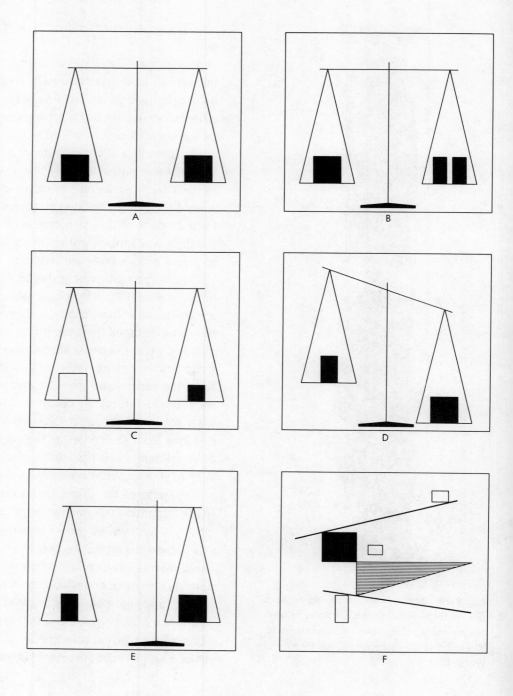

which is 4″ x 4″ at the base and 10 inches high might weigh less than a block of ebony which is 2″ x 2″ at the base and 6 inches high. It is the association that we have with size that causes us to *imagine* that the larger object is heavier. If one were planning a composition where the viewer was not going to handle the various parts of the design, the visual appearance only would be used as a guide in organizing the elements so that they appeared well balanced.

In (*f*) a variety of lines and shapes in varying degrees of darkness and lightness has been arranged in a complex informally balanced design. We need to use the eye as a gauge in shifting the parts around in the composition to determine whether they *appear* to be balanced. We cannot put them on a scale and weigh them.

In general, we associate warmer colors, brighter intensities, and darker values with a feeling of more weight. Therefore, we would plan to arrange the units of the design so the form of the colors could be utilized to advantage in determining the correct balance. The heavier forms of colors would be used in smaller areas or closer to the center, or in the lower parts of the design. If it is a three-dimensional design, the heavier forms of colors would no doubt be placed further from the front.

Informal or asymmetrical balance is sometimes referred to as active or dynamic because of the variety of ways in which an area may be organized. It is more difficult for the person untrained in art to develop a sensitivity for the beautiful casual spontaneity expressed in informal balance. Actually, when we view a room in which there is a functional arrangement of a storage piece beside a desk, or a table and lamp beside a chair, or any other arrangement planned for use, we can see a reason for not having identical forms on both sides of the design. But when we see a picture placed off-center in a wall space or a flower arrangement which is high on one side and low on the other, there may be present that quality of strangeness which is difficult at first to appreciate fully. We cannot "see" how the design achieves its equilibrium. But the unusual arrangement tends to arouse our curiosity and set us thinking.

During the last generation there have been many changes in our homes. There has been especially great change from formal living to the more informal. This difference is not only evident in ways we entertain but in the way we live. Informality has also moved into business and other

Fig. 2-25 *A,* identical objects placed equal distances from the center create formal, bisymmetrical balance; *B,* two small objects balance one large object when placed equal distances from the center—obvious formal balance; *C,* small dark object balances large light object when placed equal distances from the center; *D,* large dark object is too heavy to balance the smaller dark object if both are the same distance from the center; *E,* large dark object placed closer to the center balances the smaller dark object placed further from the center—informal balance; *F,* Variety of sizes and values of objects can be arranged to give the effect of equal weights in informal balance.

walks of life. People working in group dynamics have discovered that discussion takes place better in an informal situation than when the leader stands at the head of a room and all of the furniture faces the front. Informal situations have shown us that we feel more at ease, feel more a part of what is going on in informal situations.

This stress on informality has influenced the designer, or maybe vice versa. In most situations we feel that informal design may create more dramatic situations. The design that is planned with informal design, then, has become more accepted and a part of present-day living. Each designer must decide if he wishes to produce formal or informal design. This decision must depend on the use of his design, as well as on the personality of the designer. See Figs. 2-26, 27, and 28 for examples of formal and informal balance.

As a new design student, you must also become sensitive to the fact that informal design is not just scattering the design haphazardly. Often the person who has not developed sensitivity to informal design may be guilty of making his design a hodgepodge. You must develop an awareness to both approaches to balance and then decide which you will use in each design problem.

The two pieces of sculpture shown in Fig. 2-29a and b illustrate suggestions of formal and informal balance. The "Family Unity" shown in (a) shows the parents placed on either side of the child. The figures are not identical but are similar enough to suggest *formal balance*. The "Environmental Jewelry" shown in Fig. 2-29b is a beautiful example of subtle balancing of units to suggest *informal balance*. The two figures on the left balance the one figure and the circular disc on the right. The rods at the base on which the figures are standing are placed at various points of overlapping to aid the feeling of balance and also to present more interesting proportions.

EMPHASIS

Every design needs some note of interest that catches the eye or arrests the attention. This quality may be referred to as the *center of interest, point of emphasis,* or *dominant area.* It involves the principle of

42

Fig. 2-26 The variation in thickness of the glass in the Orefors vase provides a pleasant example of informal balance. (Photograph courtesy of Zacho, Inc.)

Fig. 2-27 A hand-blown vase of Orefors crystal expresses formal balance in the colored glass center with the thick, clear glass of the outer part. (Photograph courtesy of Zacho, Inc.)

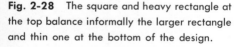

Fig. 2-28 The square and heavy rectangle at the top balance informally the larger rectangle and thin one at the bottom of the design.

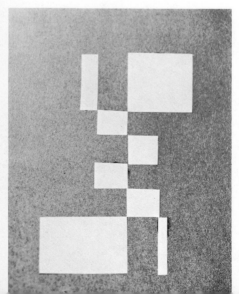

design which leads the eye first to the most important part of the design and then to other subordinating areas in the order of their importance. It is implied that there will be several centers of interest—which is true—although one will be more dominant than the others and will arrest the attention longer and draw the eye back to itself more frequently than will the lesser centers of interest. Otherwise, there would be competing areas of emphasis which would no doubt cause confusion.

WHAT TO EMPHASIZE

We need to be aware of the many possibilities of what to emphasize. In a room arrangement, a window area, a grouping of sofa, tables, and accessories, or a fireplace wall might have attention directed toward them. In an ensemble, an unusual construction arrangement of seams or interesting decorative detail, or a beautiful accessory, such as a hat, scarf, or bag, might be made the center of attraction. It might easily be one way of drawing attention away from an undesirable figure irregularity.

HOW TO EMPHASIZE

There are several ways in which we may attract attention to the important part of a design. Some of these are:

1. By use of contrasts of hue, value, or intensity
2. By leading lines
3. By unusual detail
4. By grouping or placing of objects

Sometimes several of these methods might be combined in a single design.

The eye is quickly attracted by strong contrast of dark and light, bright and dull, or by contrasts of hue if they are also decidedly different in value. Bright red letters on a bright blue background would be contrasting in hue but would vibrate too much and be difficult to read because of their

43

A

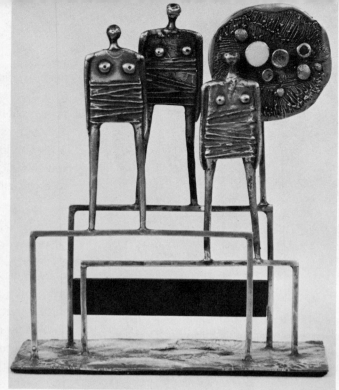

B

close value relationship. But if dark red letters were used on a light blue background they would still be contrasting in hue, and would be much easier to read because of the lack of vibration. The dark red would command more attention, whereas the light blue would be subordinated to it.

One is also conscious of the heaviness of **boldface** type as compared to *lightface* to call attention to a phrase or paragraph. Especially in advertising for magazines, posters, or display purposes, lines are employed in different ways to direct one's attention to centers of interest. In a magazine advertisement or poster, lines of various widths may break up the background space and lead the eye to the most important and then to lesser points of interest and also give a decorative quality to the advertisement. For display purposes, rods, paper streamers, ribbons, and various other materials may be used to advantage to give a line effect to draw the attention to a particular part of the display. In our discussion of the principle of proportion we mentioned the advisability of using lines in this

44

Fig. 2-29A "Family Unity" (epoxy resin sculpture, 9 feet tall) suggests formal balance. (Made by Joseph Falsetti, Associate Professor of Home Economics, University of Missouri.)

Fig. 2-29B "Environmental Jewelry." Cast silver suggests informal balance. Four inches tall. (Made by Francis Stephen, Associate Professor of Art, Texas Technological College. Photograph by Randy Miller.)

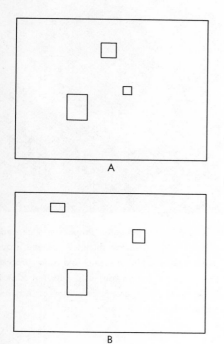

Fig. 2-30 The three centers of interest should be so arranged that the eye is carried easily from the most important to the least, and vice versa. In B the least important leads the eye out of the design.

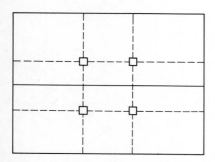

Fig. 2-31 The main center of interest should usually be located a bit above or below, a bit to the right or to the left of the center, horizontally and vertically.

way so that they would direct one's attention to the important part of the arrangement rather than to the corners of the page or window.

No doubt many of us have had the experience of passing by a window where was displayed an unusual color, suit, picture, or accessory to which we turned to give a second and longer look. The fact that it was not the usual color to which we were accustomed, or the typical convertible collar on the suit, or the familiar scene in the picture was cause enough for us to be attracted more strongly to the unusual. This quality of unusualness may be one of beauty or grotesqueness, an amusing caricature, or unusual size, shape, or texture, or decorative pattern. The fact that it is something out of the ordinary is sufficient to attract our attention to it and make it seem important.

A dynamic character due to the compact arrangement of a number of items in a group may be more effective than if each part were displayed by itself. A rhythmic quality of leading one's attention in a progressive manner to the important part of a composition requires a definite awareness of beautiful proportions. We use the term "center of interest" with no intention of placing the emphasis literally in the center. By placing it a bit to the right or left of center, and a bit above or below the center we arrive at a much more effective location for the main "point" of emphasis. In progressing easily to other subordinated areas of interest and arriving back again at the dominant one requires a "path" over which the eye may travel in an easily connected manner. The problem is not to place the least dominant center of interest so near the edge of a composition that it will be likely to lead the attention *out* of the picture rather than back to the main area of attraction (see Fig. 2-30a and b). The main center of interest should usually be located a bit above or below, a bit to the right or to the left of the center, horizontally and vertically as indicated in Fig. 2-31.

In Fig. 2-32 the free-form shape of the ashtray is more pleasing in proportion than a perfectly round form would be, and the addition of the off-center placement of the white dot adds satisfactory emphasis.

The abstract composition of the machine applique shown in Fig. 2-33 is an interesting example of eye movement from the main center of interest in the double rectangle in the lower left area, up through the horizontal and vertical rectangles in the circular "moon," and back again to the main center of interest by way of the heavy vertical line or "trunk" in the upper right area. The contrast of dark and light in the lower area naturally causes a more dramatic emphasis on this part of the design. The overlapping of free-form shapes gives the illusion of space and leads the eye into the composition.

In Fig. 2-34 the abstract portrayal of "The Last Supper" illustrates very vividly how the center of interest *may* be satisfactorily placed directly in the center of the composition. Note, however, the informal irregularity of the placement of the other figures on opposite sides of the central figure of Christ—five on one side and six on the other, for more interesting proportion. The portrayal leaves much to the imagination of the viewer. For instance, each viewer could supply the facial features, the folds of the drapery in the garments, and other details that would present a more realistic interpretation. Even the fact that one disciple is missing causes the viewer to wonder and question. The one looking at the composition must involve himself with it in order to add in his own imagination whatever other details he wishes to add to be able to enjoy it to the fullest.

Mounting a picture on a background shape or planning a mat for it are problems in proportion, balance, and in emphasis. One needs to plan the width of margins to be pleasing in relation to each other. The picture is to be viewed on the wall in a vertical position, and therefore one needs to plan the bottom margin wider than the other three for better balance (see Fig. 2-35). If they were all the same, the "Law of Optics" would make the picture appear to be sliding down in space. From the standpoint of emphasis, we need a rectangular shape of background on which to place the rectangular picture in order to emphasize the picture and not the background. A rectangular frame for a rectangular picture will not compete with the shape of the picture as would an oval frame for a rectangular picture. If the object is to be viewed in a flat position or from all sides like a tablecloth on a table, then the opposite sides should be the same size and should be parallel with the table. Placing a cloth diagonally on a table is contrary to the shape of the table and there is lack of emphasis on the cloth in relation to the table. Mounting a picture on a background might not always necessitate leaving identical margins on each side. In Fig. 2-36 the dark square on the left not only balances informally the mass

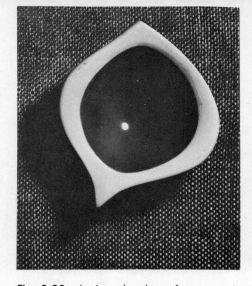

Fig. 2-32 An irregular shape for a ceramic ashtray with irregular thickness of the sides expresses imagination and pleasing proportions. (Made by Howard Kilns, Staten Island, New York. Photograph courtesy of Raymor Manufacturing Division.)

Fig. 2-33 Placing the gray and black shapes in the lower left area attracts one's attention first; then the line to the right leads our eyes to other subordinating areas. (Made by Dr. Foster Marlow, Head; Dept. of Art, Southwest Texas State College.)

Fig. 2-34 The abstract portrayal of "The Last Supper" shows the center of interest directly in the center, but with other subordinating figures placed in informal irregularity on either side for more interesting proportion. (Owned by Dr. Bill C. Lockhart.)

of lines on the right but also serves as the accent or note of emphasis in the composition.

RHYTHM

A sense of order, a quality of gracefulness, a feeling of easy movement—all lead to a principle of design which we may call "rhythm." All of us may tingle to the tips of our toes when we watch the graceful, lithe, movements of a ballet dancer as she pirouettes, spins, and leaps. If she appears clumsy in her movements, it may be because of lack of skill, but it also shows an absence of a feeling for beautiful *rhythmic* movement.

Rhythm is related movement or this sense of leading the eye easily from one part of a design to another in an easy, flowing manner. We say that a certain design shows rhythm, but it is not in the individual shapes, but in the change from one line to another, from one dimension to another, from one color to another, one value to another. In music, it isn't that each sound is rhythmical but rather it is the change from one sound to another with the proper amount of time elapse between each note, or the change in pitch of each note that creates the rhythm. Sounds like a drum beat can become rhythmical when the beats are rapid at times and slow at others, arranged in a semblance of order or a "certain time." On the other hand, the notes might be all timed the same, but they may vary in pitch.

REPETITION

We may express a feeling of rhythm by *repetition* of lines, colors, and shapes, but in so doing we must also keep in mind the principles of proportion that deal with unity, with a certain amount of variety to add interest (see Fig. 2-37a). Shapes that are all the same size and shape with the same spacing between each would give us an example of repetition, but it might be very monotonous. In Fig. 2-37b the same shapes have been placed unequal distances apart for a more subtle rhythmical "beat." Properly organized shapes for a background for wallpaper, allover fabric

(below left)
Fig. 2-35A If an object is to be viewed from the top or from all sides, the margins are usually the same on opposite sides, and the object harmonizes in shape with the background.

(below center)
Fig. 2-35B If an object is to be viewed in a vertical position, the bottom margin is usually wider than the other three.

(below right)
Fig. 2-35C A design may be planned with the emphasis off-center for a more dramatic effect.

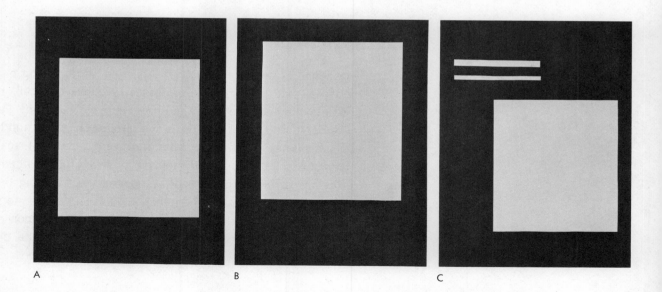

A   B   C

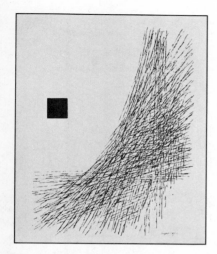

Fig. 2-36 Mass of lines organized to informally balance the dark square. "Accent" by Herbert Bayer. (Courtesy of Container Corporation of America.)

design, or floor covering might show a definite regular repeat in order to keep the design "in the background." But a design for a more dramatic effect, as in a roomdivider, may show more irregularity of spacing for pleasing rhythm (see Fig. 2-38).

GRADATION OR PROGRESSION

A gradual change in the length or thickness of lines may give variety, but if it is so obvious that one is striving for *gradation* or *progression*, it, too, would become monotonous. Besides a gradual change in length or thickness of lines, one may seek variety in a change in spacing between lines, or shapes; change in hue, value, or intensity; change in amounts overlapped in a composition; change in texture from smooth to rough, shiny to dull. (See Figs. 2-39*a* and *b*.)

In Fig. 2-40 the ever-widening circular movement of the structure of the shell produces a feeling of rhythm. Also the faintly radiating lines in the opposite direction lengthwise of the shell add a graceful delicacy as contrasted by the heavy, stubby "fingerlike" projections around the sides. Nature has a way of combining heaviness and daintiness in her own inimitable way. Look at the heavy trunk of a tree, the small branches and

(near right)
Fig. 2-37A Shapes may be repeated, but they may make a rather monotonous arrangement if they are all the same size and same distance apart.

(far right)
Fig. 2-37B Even though the shapes are identical, they can give a more pleasing rhythmical pattern when the spaces between them are varied.

A   B

twigs, and then the dainty lines of the veins of the leaves. And yet they all blend together to give a rhythmical harmony unsurpassed in the man-made objects of the world.

We usually think of rhythm as expressing a quality of lithesome grace, but this does not exclude the dramatic slashes of a Voodoo dancer or the rapid zigzag of a lightning flash. These express other kinds of rhythm that show more speed, but they might still express repetition, gradation, or continuous line movement. The shell illustrated in Fig. 2-41 shows a graceful example of irregular gradation in the fingerlike projections at its base. In Fig. 2-42 the gradation of sizes of figures in the foreground has not been arranged in stair-step fashion and thus presents a pleasant example of rhythm. The sharp triangular figures with their even more sharply pointed background shadows express this more dramatic form or rhythm mentioned above.

CONTINUOUS RELATED MOVEMENT

In some designs it is not evident that any elements are repeated, or that there is a progressive change from one part of the design to another,

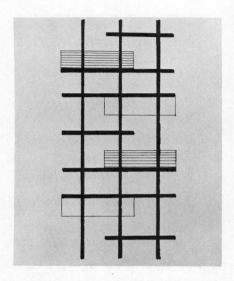

Fig. 2-38 Besides having the spaces varied between shapes, other decorative details, such as the thin and heavy lines, might be added.

A   B

(*far left*)
Fig. 2-39A Shapes may be graduated in size, but when they are much the same in shape and the gradation is too obvious, the design becomes monotonous.

(*near left*)
Fig. 2-39B A more dramatic effect can be produced by more subtle gradation.

and yet we have a sense of easy movement throughout the design. See Fig. 2-43. This related movement may be literally in a *continuous line*. It may be in a *suggestion* of a continuous line, occasionally having breaks in the line but spaces that are small enough so the eye still carries over to the next section of the line in a rhythmical manner. (See Figs. 2-44, 45, and 46.) The movement may be in a series of lines within lines as in growth rings of a tree trunk or grain lines in a plank of wood. We may call this "continuous related movement" which produces a

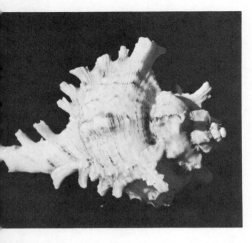

Fig. 2-40 Natural rhythm expressed in the ever-widening circular movement of the shell's structure.

Fig. 2-41 Natural rhythm in the irregular gradation of the fingerlike projections at the base of the shell.

Fig. 2-42 The variation in height of the figures in the foreground and the dark spires of the Cathedral in the background create a graceful rhythm throughout the tapestry. ("Cathedral," tapestry designed by Martta Taipole. Photograph courtesy of the American Crafts Council.)

Fig. 2-43 The gradation of size of the triangles of white walrus tusk and the continuous line movement of the grain of the wood lead the eye in a rhythmical manner. Wood carving by George Federoff. (Photograph courtesy of the American Crafts Council.)

feeling of rhythm. In the flowing lines of an Oriental garment we may see a beautiful example of continuous related movement throughout the entire garment. In Fig. 2-47 note how the corrugated paper has been arranged in a graceful continuous line rhythm.

HARMONY

Some designers will include a fifth principle of design, that of *harmony*. It is the opinion of the authors that if the principles of proportion, balance, emphasis, and rhythm are applied creatively so that there is a sense of beauty in the design, the resulting attribute will be that of harmony or unity. It is a culminating goal toward which we are striving when we select and arrange the various elements of design for a particular purpose. If we have failed to apply any one of the principles of design, then the resulting design will also lack harmony.

Let us use a particular design (Fig. 2-48) to consider the ways in which the various principles of design have been planned in relation to it. *Informal balance* has been used, with different "tree" shapes placed different distances from the center but so neither side seems to be heavier than the other nor have a greater power of attraction. Sufficient dark value and larger shapes have been used in the lower part to give a feeling of stability, and yet there is also some dark value in smaller amounts in the upper part to carry the eye upward and balance the whole composition.

Fig. 2-44 The terra cotta wall plaque expresses rhythm by means of a beautiful continuous line movement throughout the design. (Photograph courtesy of Design Today, Inc.)

Fig. 2-45 Student sketch of continuous related line movement. (Photograph by Randy Miller.)

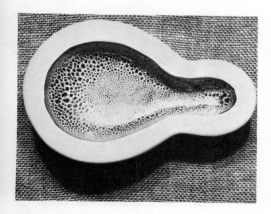

Fig. 2-46 The "iron spots" in the glaze of the base of the ceramic ashtray express a subtle gradation of size, creating a rhythmical pattern. (Designer, Harding Black. Photograph courtesy of Design Today, Inc.)

Unity with variety in the *proportions* has been achieved. The "tree" shapes are all triangles, but they vary both in size and in the decorative manner in which the space is broken in each one. *Emphasis* has been placed on the small figures of the elk by making them dark in value and surrounding them with a light background. The "trees" are also clustered around them to center attention on them. *Rhythm* has been attained by means of repetition, gradation, and continuous line movement. There is gradation of size of the triangular shapes from the small ones at the top to the large ones at the base. They have the same basic shape, even though each "tree" has a different decorative pattern of "branches." A feeling of continuous line movement has been achieved by overlapping the shapes in differing amounts so the eye is led in a rhythmical path from one shape to the next. The straight lines of the "trunks" also lead the eye from the base of the panel to the top. The composition lends itself to its use as a decorative wall panel. Thus, because all the principles of design have been applied appropriately, we can assume there is *harmony* in the composition. The lack of harmony would enter into the problem if one used this design inappropriately as a wall panel with formal traditional furnishings. It suggests an informal contemporary setting.

In Figs. 2-49 and 50 see further comparisons of grouping of figures.

It is true that too much "academic" application of the principles of design can sometimes cause the design to become stiff and lacking in

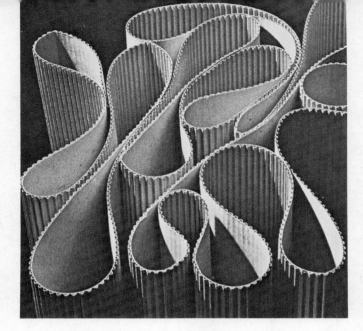

Fig. 2-47 Corrugated paper organized in a continuous line pattern which expresses rhythm. (Courtesy of Container Corporation of America.)

spontaneity. A design is not necessarily good just because we set out to deliberately achieve balance, pleasing proportion, or locate a center of interest. It may be the result of much searching, experimentation, and many trials. The final design may have been done quickly and with little effort, but it takes as much practice and skill as a musician would use in learning to play a concerto.

Under the pretense of harmony one can carry an idea to the extreme. For instance, it is possible to carry association of ideas so far that it becomes ridiculous, as when a steak platter is decorated with a bright red steak or a preserve jar is shaped like a strawberry with a cluster of leaves and a stem for the handle. Our problem is to train ourselves to recognize the significant and creative from the commonplace and faddish.

Our tastes are developed through study, observation, association, and experience. In a course such as this book suggests, we are exposed to a discussion of terms pertaining to design. We create designs ourselves and observe demonstrations or watch techniques with which fellow classmates experiment. Thus we grow in our sensitivity toward the organization of the principles of design so that the resulting attribute will be *harmony*.

Fig. 2-48 A more subtle gradation in size, and dark and light have been used in the "Forest" with a different decorative design planned for each tree (designed by Ethel Jane Beitler).

Fig. 2-49 Poorly organized grouping of figures. Spacing between figures is too similar. Reflections produce monotonous bisymmetrical balance. Figures are equally emphasized. No creative thinking applied to the arrangement.

Fig. 2-50 Well organized grouping of figures. One figure on left placed by itself and two on the right placed together suggest more interesting proportions. The two figures attract more emphasis to the group with the single figure showing satisfactory subordination. The lighting is planned to eliminate the confusing shadow treatment shown in Fig. 2-49. (Figures owned by Dr. Bill C. Lockhart.)

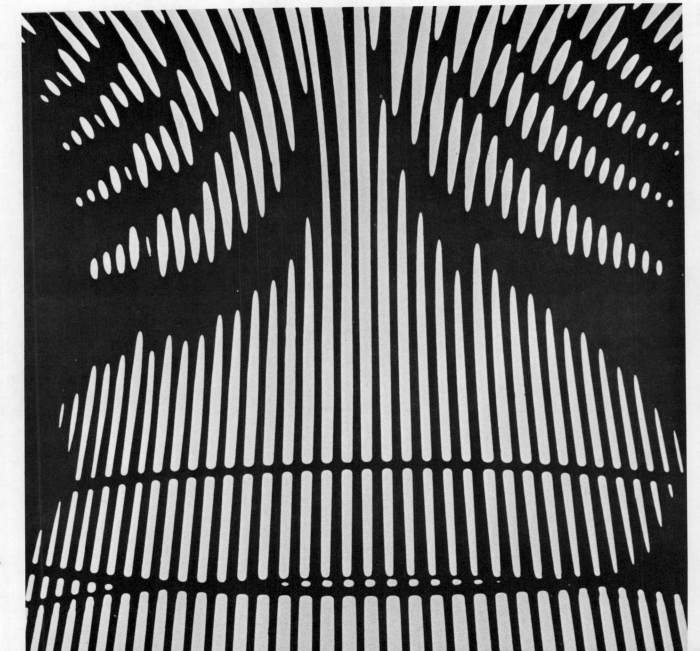

3

WHAT'S YOUR LINE?

On a piece of paper we make a mark that causes our eyes to move from one end of the mark to the other. We call such a mark a "line." Rathbun and Hayes in *Layman's Guide to Modern Art* state: "Line is an abstraction; there are boundaries but no actual lines in nature. Objects merely come to an end and other objects begin, but the painter represents this fact by a line." Line has only one major dimension—length—but may move in any direction. The width or thickness of line may introduce a second dimension. However, it is debatable as to how thick a line may be before it becomes identified as a shape. See Fig. 3-1 for an exciting study of a detail of a stool. Actually the element of line is emphasized more than that of shape.

CHARACTERISTICS OF LINES

All lines fall into the category of straight, curved, or a combination of these two. This may produce wavy, scalloped, or zigzag lines. Lines can basically move in a vertical, horizontal, or diagonal direction, or a combination of any of these (see Fig. 3-2). Physical characteristics of lines may be described as thick, thin, smooth, fuzzy, long, short, as well as many others. The various tools, materials, and techniques used to create lines

Fig. 3-1 Detail of a stool designed by Warren Platner shows an interesting line pattern. (Courtesy of Knoll Associates, Inc.)

will help determine these physical characteristics. (See photographs on pages 76 to 81 for examples of experiments with lines, using a variety of tools, materials, and techniques.) The expressive character of the line may be defined as exciting, quiet, dignified, angry, active, or happy. The expressive character of a line is the result of its direction and physical qualities as interpreted by the designer or the viewer.

In order to enjoy life to the utmost, one needs to be continually observing with rapt attentiveness even the smallest details of his environment. If we have trained ourselves to notice, we will be more inclined to notice everything—not just the design of a garment and the color and texture of the fabric, but the least irregularity of hemline, or unevenness of stitching in a seam. Of course we will note not only the unsatisfactory items but also the many points of beauty. We mentioned earlier that "there are boundaries but no actual lines in nature." However, if we regard a scene from nature with attention, we begin to see where lines are *suggested* by the curving waves, the rolling hills, or waving grain. We could put a sheet of tracing paper over a photograph of a natural form and sketch a pattern of lines. These suggestions of lines are everywhere about us if we will only open our eyes and enjoy their beauty. Following are only a few examples:

1. The irregular, dashing lines made by the waves as they lap the shore-line.
2. The lines made by the branches of the trees as they reach upward toward the sky.
3. The undulating movements of waving grain and grasses as they sway in the breeze.
4. The lacy pattern of veins in a leaf.
5. The radiating lines made by a clump of iris leaves.
6. The lines cut into the snow from tire treads or the marks of the chains.
7. The pattern of lines in a picket fence, a venetian blind, a striped or plaid fabric.
8. The composition of vertical and horizontal lines made by the steel framework of a building under construction.
9. The suggestion of irregular parallel lines in the grain of a beautiful piece of wood.

58

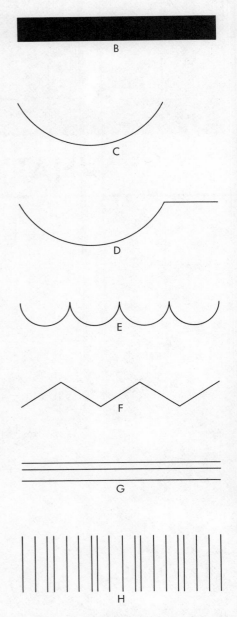

Fig. 3-2 *A,* straight line; *B,* is it a line or a shape? *C,* curved line; *D,* straight and curved lines combined; *E,* scalloped line; *F,* zigzag line; *G,* horizontal line; *H,* vertical lines.

Fig. 3-3 Freehand lines were made with a brush and tempera paint. Note the manner in which the lines have been organized in a "unit" and the unit repeated as a border.

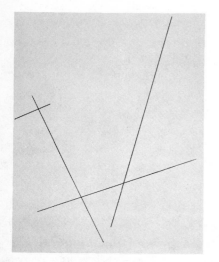

Fig. 3-4 The exact or "ruler-precise" lines show variety in length, direction, and spacing.

10. The graceful stream of white vapor trail from a jet plane as it whizzes through space.

An individual can develop a sensitivity to the beauty of the element of line in unplanned design and design in nature. Then it would become easier to go one step further and create interesting line patterns of his own. There are times when a simple arrangement of thick and thin, long and short, fuzzy and smooth will satisfy our need for decoration—just an interesting line pattern, with no attempt to represent an animal, a bird, or other object. It is sometimes wise to break away from the mathematically precise arrangement of lines which look as though each had been drawn with a ruler and the space between measured accurately. One of the secrets of the element of line is the recognition that it is possible to achieve beauty with a *planned* form of irregularity, rather than with the careless irregularity due to a lack of skill or planning. (Compare the preciseness or irregularity in Figs. 3-3 and 3-4.)

To some, the wrinkles that have developed in the brown and leathered face of a ninety-year-old grandmother mean nothing as far as age is concerned. They represent, rather, the beauty of lines that suggest the "living" that she has enjoyed over the years. The laugh lines radiating from the corners of the eyes and mouth, the anxiety lines in the forehead, the calligraphy of lines throughout her cheeks and chin—all express

59

beauty of soul to those who love her. (Compare the ages expressed by the lines in Figs. 3-5 and 3-6.)

The homeowner cannot help but be annoyed with the persistent growth of dandelions in his yard. But let a nice big one go to seed, and we must admit that the lacy, fuzzy lines suggested by the beautiful head is the most fragile calligraphy of lines imaginable. Harry Bertoia recognized that beauty when he created his six-foot sculpture of the "dandelion gone to seed." (See Figs. 3-7 and 3-8.)

Occasionally an artist becomes more known for his line compositions than for any other quality. Paul Klee, for instance, has an amusing way with lines, making just a few of them express a mood or represent a child-like figure (see Fig. 3-9).

Physical qualities of lines refer mainly to the general character of lines used for a particular kind of representation. For instance, if we were attempting to represent an object against a background, we could suggest a sense of space so much more effectively by using sharp lines in the foreground and fuzzy or woolly ones in the background.

Impressions of daintiness, boldness, or gracefulness may be *suggested* by fine lines, heavy lines, or curved ones respectively. In the fashion sketch (Fig. 3-10) the rendering has been developed with fine pencil strokes, expressing a quality of refinement. One might also note the easy, free quality expressed by the technique of the designer. Occasionally letting a line fade out, or leaving a blank space in the sketching of a line takes away the tightness or stiffness that might otherwise be expressed by means of a continuous contour line. The ends of the lines are close enough together that the eye can easily fill in the spaces. It may be compared to two lines that do not touch but suggest a right angle. When something is left to the imagination, the effect is more interesting than if all the details are complete. In listening to music, the occasional pause is more pleasing than the continuous sound of the melody. Our ears pick up the tune easily and go on.

Note in Figs. 3-11 and 3-12 other expressive characteristics of lines. In Fig. 3-11 the dainty lines have been intertwined around the bold lines to express motion. In Fig. 3-12 the lines seem to span a space.

Straight lines express *force*. The fact that a line has no curves or bends in it indicates a forcefulness and strength necessary to keep it straight.

Fig. 3-5 A rhythmical line drawing of an elderly woman, showing calligraphy of lines. (Student sketch. Photograph by Randy Miller.)

Fig. 3-6 A dramatic line drawing of a middle-aged woman. Note fewer lines around the eyes, nose, and mouth than in the one above. (Student sketch. Photograph by Randy Miller.)

Fig. 3-7 "The Dandelion," six feet tall, by Harry Bertoia, was not designed necessarily to resemble a dandelion but to be a spherical form which would enable one to look inside. The beautiful line pattern looks so fragile one might be afraid to touch it. (Owners, Mr. and Mrs. Harry Hood Bassett. Photograph by Herbert Matter. Reprinted from Vogue, copyright 1959, The Condé Nast Publications, Inc.)

Fig. 3-8 The fragileness of the actual "dandelion gone to seed" also suggests a beautiful calligraphy of lines.

Fig. 3-9 The amusing charm of the few simple lines used by Paul Klee in his painting "Nearly Hit" produced a story of a narrow escape. (Photograph courtesy of San Francisco Museum of Art. Albert M. Bender collection.)

When we lie down to rest, we assume a horizontal position; therefore, horizontal lines suggest repose and calmness. When we are standing or walking, we are in a vertical position, and consequently, vertical lines express activity. When we run, the legs, body, and arms assume more of a zigzag position, and the speed of running expresses more excitement and movement. The zigzag lines of lightning cannot help but make you *excited* as you view the rapid irregular line of light in the sky.

These three ways of denoting expressiveness and physical qualities of line are quite evident in the three sketches of horses. (See Figs. 3-13, 3-14, and 3-15.) In each sketch one can discern that a horse is *represented*, even though in an abstract manner. In the first sketch the lines are refined and are more delicate and sharp, *suggesting* the speed of a racehorse. In the second the lines are varied in thickness, but the predominance of thick lines *suggests* a heavy workhorse. The third is sketched in a highly *decorative* manner with a continuous line pattern to appeal to the aesthetic emotions of the viewer. It shows a playful, fun-loving character on the part of the designer.

To be truly beautiful a line must appear to have some purpose. It must "go someplace" rather than meander aimlessly all over the space. The director of a large high school once cautioned his staff members, "If you find it necessary to leave your classrooms on an errand, walk as though you were going someplace with a purpose, and then if a board member or I happen to see you out of your classroom, we'll know it is a necessary absence from duty!" And so, with your lines—we can make them appear weak and uncertain of their destination, or we can make them strong, dynamic and purposeful. See Figs. 3-16a and b. Note the purposeful lines of the four-level interchange shown in Fig. 3-17. Fig. 3-18 is a free-brush line which has been planned purposely to indicate "depression."

Persons who make a study of handwriting like to suggest that it is possible to determine personality traits, state of one's health, criminal tendencies, and a host of other characteristics by the way in which we cross our "t's," shape our "m's," or run our letters together. The story

Fig. 3-10 In representing a fashion sketch, lines are made faint or thin on the side which shows highlights and made heavy on the shadow side. Lines enable us to determine the details of the garment. (Student sketch. Photograph by Randy Miller.)

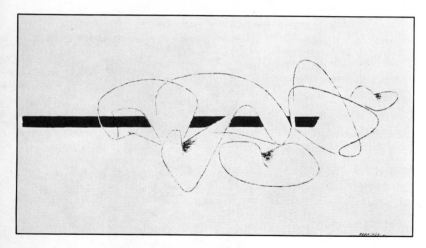

Fig. 3-11   Lines organized to express motion. They also express boldness and daintiness because of the contrast of thickness and thinness. ("Motion Along a Horizontal" by Herbert Bayer; courtesy of Container Corporation of America.)

Fig. 3-13   Racehorse.

Fig. 3-14   Workhorse.

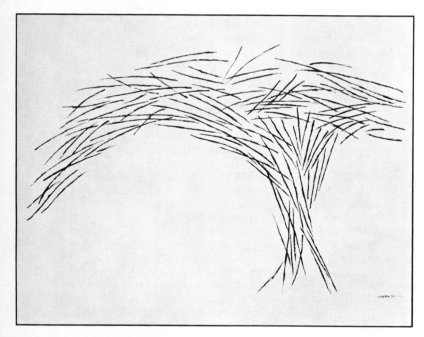

Fig. 3-12   Lines organized to express expansion over a space. "Span" by Herbert Bayer. (Courtesy of Container Corporation of America.)

Fig. 3-15   Decorative horse.

is told that Abraham Lincoln, as he prepared to sign the Emancipation Proclamation, twice picked up his pen and put it down. Then he turned to William E. Seward, his Secretary of State, and said, "I have been shaking hands since nine o'clock this morning and my right arm is almost paralyzed. If my name ever goes into history, it will be for this act, and my whole soul is in it. If my hand trembles when I sign the Proclamation, all who examine the document hereafter will say, 'He hesitated.' "He then turned to the table, took up the pen again, and slowly, firmly, wrote, "Abraham Lincoln."

Study the lines used in the abstract design of the church shown in Fig. 3-19. The lines are not especially heavy, but have a quality of stability and strength due to the tall, straight verticals and diagonals. The two designs using curved lines shown in Figs. 3-20 and 3-21 express a decidedly different character, due perhaps to their thickness. Each is composed of relatively short, curved lines, but in Fig. 3-20 the lines are organized in a dramatic combination of sizes with interesting placement, providing rest spaces. In Fig. 3-21 a more Oriental effect has been achieved by the suggestion of branches and no apparent horizon line.

In block-printing, the design is sometimes referred to as a "black-line" or a "white-line" depending upon the areas carved out of the block. In

Fig. 3-16 Bold lines as expressed by the four-level interchange at Fort Worth, Texas. (Photograph courtesy of Texas Highway Department.)

A   B

Fig. 3-17 *A,* an unorganized line design; *B,* an organized line design.

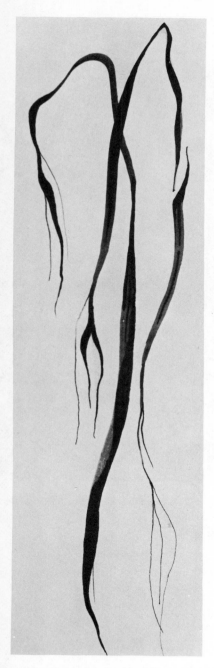

Fig. 3-18 A free-brush and ink line expresses "depression."

Fig. 3-19 Vertical and diagonal lines produce a quality of strength and stability. (Student design.)

Fig. 3-20 Short, curved lines, alternately repeated in direction, produce a strong dramatic effect. (Student design.)

Fig. 3-21 More delicate curved lines are used to produce a graceful Oriental effect. (Student design.)

Fig. 3-23 the shapes are outlines with the cut-out part of the block giving an example of a "white-line" design. (This is true also of the rubber cement design shown in Fig. 3-50.) If the composition in Fig. 3-22 had been printed from a linoleum block, it would be classified as a "black-line" design because the major portion of the area would be carved out, leaving only the lines to print.

PURPOSES OF LINES

TO CREATE A SHAPE

The most frequently used type of line is that of the "outline." More on this point will be discussed later in the chapter on *Shape*, although

Fig. 3-23 The cut-out parts of the blockprint produce a ''white-line'' design.

Fig. 3-22 Variation in thickness of brush strokes provide character and depth of emotion in a ''black-line'' design. (Designer, Margaret Stiles.)

here it might be stated that the shape of the object would be indicated by bringing the ends of the line together. For instance, a line may be curved so much that the opposite ends meet and form a circle or oval. Four lines the same length may be touched at the ends to form a square. From these simple illustrations we may go on to recognize the use of lines to define the shape of a human figure, an animal, a building, or any particular object. The degree to which these lines are exaggerated in length or direction may indicate the degree of abstraction or realism that may be represented in the design. In Fig. 3-24 note the way in which the lengths of copper wire are bent and welded together to suggest the female figure. No attempt has been made to represent in a realistic way the individual features of eyes, nose, mouth, hair, and yet there is no question of the intent of the designer. In Fig. 3-25 angular pen lines suggest buildings, hills, trees, boats, or whatever one wishes to imagine the lines represent. There may be sufficient ''likeness'' in a design for us to be able to use descriptive adjectives in relation to the lines. For instance, the lines may represent a fashion sketch referred to earlier (see Fig. 3-10.)

67

The lines enable us to determine the style of neckline, sleeves, fullness of the skirt, and general type of silhouette.

Decorative or *aesthetic* qualities may be recognized in the details of the garment, as in the shape of the collar and the seam lines in the jacket. They may also be recognized in the beautiful spacing of lines between the seams.

The actual form of the design may be a linear one that creates a decorative effect. For instance, in Fig. 3-26 the form of the mobile bird sculpture is made from welded steel wires to suggest the structure of the body, neck, wings, and tail in a graceful, well-proportioned arrangement of "lines." In Fig. 3-27 the small applique from the San Blas islands emphasizes the contour line of the bird shape, and also the vertical lines suggest a decorative feature within the shape.

Fig. 3-24 The continuous length of copper wire is bent and welded together to suggest the female figure. No attempt has been made to represent in a realistic way the individual features of eyes, nose, mouth, hair, and yet there is no question of the intent of the designer to represent a female figure. (Designer, Dr. Bill C. Lockhart.)

Fig. 3-25 Angular pen lines suggest buildings, hills, trees, boats, or whatever one wishes to imagine the lines represent. (Stuart Davis, Composition Number 4, 1934. Brush and Ink, Gift of Mrs. John D. Rockefeller, Jr. Courtesy of the Museum of Modern Art.)

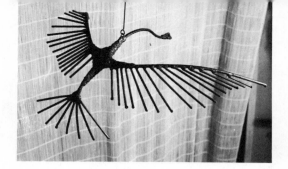

Fig. 3-26 Welding rods may be used to produce a linear type of sculpture. (Designer, Dr. Bill C. Lockhart.)

Fig. 3-27 A contour line achieved by appliqueing one fabric on another in a Mola made in the San Blas Islands.

TO CREATE A PATTERN

The continuous beat of a drum with its rapid and slow, loud and soft reverberations of sound might suggest to us a pattern of lines that could be planned for a border. Many lines close together with an occasional one spaced further away could indicate the rapid and slow beats on the drum. Broad and short lines could suggest the loud and soft beats. And so, we develop a rhythmical border (see Fig. 3-28).

Repeating our border in all directions is one way of creating an allover pattern. If designers of wallpaper or printed fabrics had no other element except line, there still could be a never-ending array of arrangements that could be made (see Fig. 3-29).

69

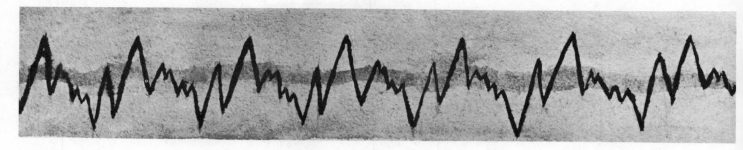

Note the various patterns illustrated in Figs. 3-30 through 3-33. Curved and straight lines, some overlapping, some basically parallel, some thick and some thin are obtained by varying pressures on the brush in different directions. The techniques used in making these patterns naturally give the lines the particular characteristics discussed earlier in this chapter.

The scratched pattern of lines for the decoration of the bowl shown in Fig. 3-34 by Ed and Mary Schier are organized in a compact border to enrich the exterior surface in an irregular, but bold and dramatic manner. On the other hand, the precise regularity of the lines in the circular pattern on the plate in Fig. 3-35 present an exciting, but elegant and formal appearance.

In the allover pattern in Chapter 4, Figs. 4-20 and 4-21, the linear shapes of the rectangles overlapping the solid shapes of other rectangles give an interesting variation to a simple geometric design.

Lettering in itself is a combination of various types of straight and curved lines, and line directions of vertical, horizontal, and diagonal. Besides this, in Fig. 3-36 the lettering has been arranged in a "line" that moves back and forth with a whiplike action for a dramatic effect. In Fig. 3-37 yarn has been used as a linear accent on the free-form background areas. Note in Fig. 3-38 how the negative areas between the shapes create a linear pattern which adds interest to the overall design.

The line designs may be enjoyed in the natural patterns in objects from nature, such as the grain lines in a piece of wood or branches of a tree or stems and leaves of a plant (see Figs. 3-39, 40, and 41). In Fig. 3-42 the photomicrograph of the transverse section of a lily anther showing the pollen chambers containing pollen grains expresses a free-form linear pattern that might give the creative person an excellent idea for a stitchery

Fig. 3-28 A rhythmical border developed from the sound of an African drum beat.

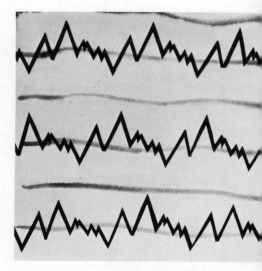

Fig. 3-29 An allover pattern developed from the border above.

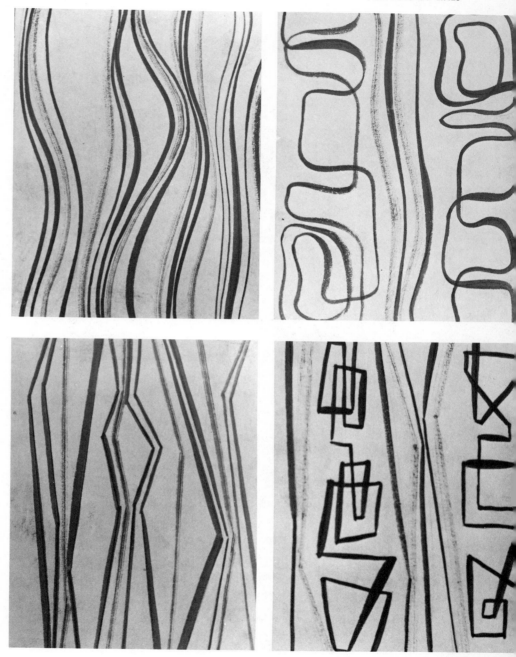

(upper left)

Fig. 3-30 Curved and straight lines were made with varying amounts of pressure put on the brush to give different widths of lines. Curves lines, not overlapping.

(upper right)

Fig. 3-31 Curves lines, with some continuous and overlapping.

(lower left)

Fig. 3-32 Relatively straight and angular lines, with none overlapping.

(lower right)

Fig. 3-33 Relatively straight and angular lines, with some continuous and overlapping.

Fig. 3-34 Contemporary hand-thrown ceramic bowl, made by Ed and Mary Schier, appropriately enriched with a scratched pattern of lines. (Courtesy of the American Crafts Council.)

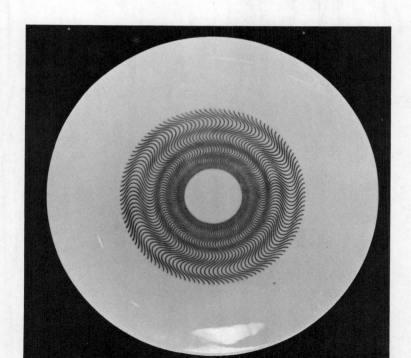

Fig. 3-35 The elegant "roulette" pattern of Arzberg porcelain shows graceful rhythm in the radiating lines. (Designer, Jean Luce.)

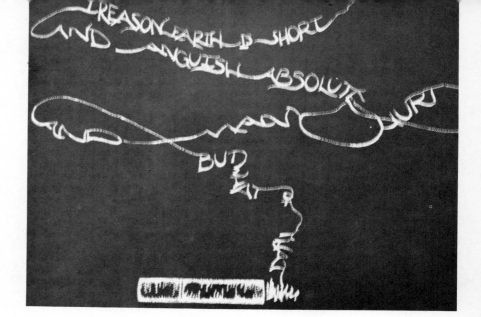

Fig. 3-36 Lettering may be made to appear more decorative when organized in a "whiplash" type of line movement. (Student design.)

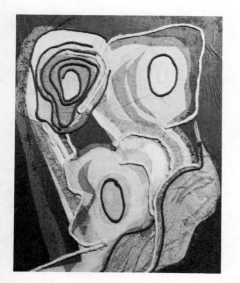

Fig. 3-37 Yarn on a tissue paper collage background gives added emphasis to a linear effect. (Student design.)

project. The same is true of the photomicrograph shown in Fig. 3-43 in the transverse section of a basswood stem. The winter and summer growth rings are clearly evident in the dark and light values. It might give a designer an idea for a lacy open-tapestry or a stitchery wallpiece.

TO DIVIDE SPACE AND CREATE MOVEMENT

Note in the section on proportion in Chapter 2 how lines may be used to divide spaces; in Chapter 2, Fig. 2-16, the lines that divide the spaces equally present a rather monotonous effect. A striped fabric in which all the lines are the same thickness with the space between all the same expresses little imagination of the designer. More exciting stripes and plaids are those that have more irregularity of spacing between the lines, and in the lines themselves. Other examples of division of space in stripes are shown in Fig. 2-16. In the wavy line stripe in Fig. 3-44 note the narrow space between the wide lines. In Fig. 3-4 the diagonal lines break the space into large, medium, and small areas. In Fig. 3-3 the freehand lines are irregularly spaced within the unit which is repeated in a border. The spaces between the lines have been kept uneven to add interest to the overall repeat.

The line pattern cut into the tire shown in Fig. 3-45 gives a feeling of continuous, linear movement both in the positive and negative lines in the tire tread, and also in the pattern of lines pressed into the snow.

TO CREATE OPTICAL ILLUSIONS

We may purposely use lines in a variety of ways to make things appear different from what they seem. The student may refer back to Chapter 2 in the discussion of the principle of proportion and the problem of creating optical illusions by means of lines. In general, we say that horizontal lines add apparant width to a shape, and vertical lines tend to carry the eye up and down and add to the height (see Fig. 3-46).

In Fig. 3-47 note the way in which the horizontal lines have been organized to create the illusion of distance. The illusion of space has been achieved by the use of horizontal lines placed closer and closer together as they progress upward in the composition.

CREATIVE EXPERIMENTS

Following are exercises that are planned to help you as a student in your understanding and appreciation of the element of line. The written information and illustrations should stimulate your ability to see and to create pleasing organizations of lines. Just reading these chapters and information in other sources cannot take the place of your continual observation and actual experimentation, using many techniques and a variety of tools and materials. You should constantly refer back, however, to the chapter on the principles of design to evaluate the arrangement of lines to determine if you have a feeling of proper balance, pleasing proportion, and effective emphasis, and graceful rhythm.

Nature offers us excellent keys to good organization in design. Man's reorganization of nature into stiff and regimented designs so often violates the natural beauty of nature. Frequently in landscaping of a garden the attempt is toward extreme formality which is in direct contrast to the pleasing informality of nature.

Fig. 3-38 Small rectangles and squares placed close together produce a linear character to the spaces between the shapes. (Student design.)

Fig. 3-39 A line design inspired from the natural grain of wood shown in *B*.

Fig. 3-40 A line design inspired from the natural radiation of branches of a tree shown in *B*.

Fig. 3-41 A line design inspired from the graceful leaves and plumes of pampas grass shown in *B*.

75

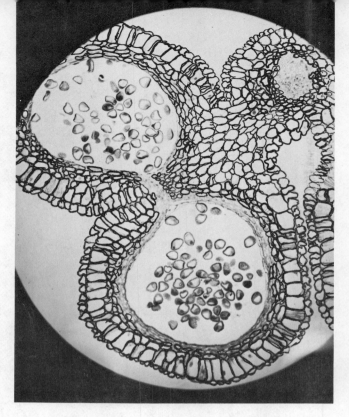

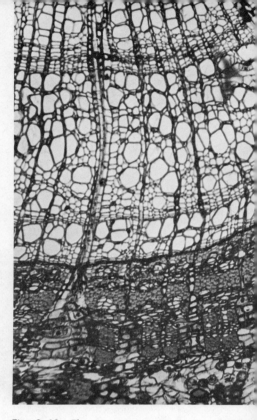

Fig. 3-42 The transverse section of a lily anther, showing the pollen chambers containing pollen grains produces a lacy linear design. (Photograph courtesy of Dr. Earl D. Camp, Chairman, Dept. of Biology, Texas Tech University.)

Fig. 3-43 The transverse section of a basswood stem also produces a variation of lacy effects. (Photograph courtesy of Dr. Earl D. Camp, Chairman, Dept. of Biology, Texas Tech University.)

The following problems may help you to explore and become more aware of the characteristics of line.

1. Find examples of various types of lines in magazine illustrations. Ask yourself the following questions in evaluating the illustrations:

    (a) In what ways do the lines reflect the character of the illustration?

    (b) In what ways do the lines fail to reflect the character of the illustration?

    (c) In what ways has variety been expressed in the lines? (Thick-

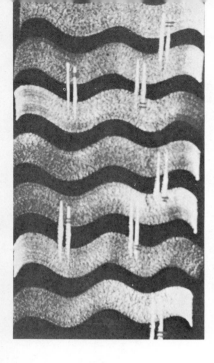

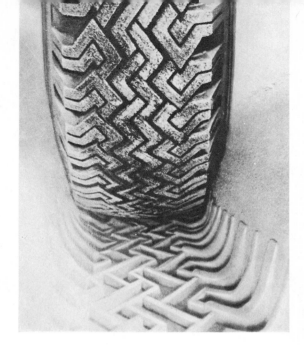

Fig. 3-45 Tire tracks in the snow make an interesting line pattern of ridges. (Photograph courtesy of Goodyear Tire and Rubber Company.)

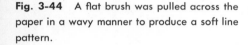

Fig. 3-44 A flat brush was pulled across the paper in a wavy manner to produce a soft line pattern.

ness, thinness, length of lines, direction of lines, straight versus curved.)

(d) Does this variety of lines lead to a unified design?

(e) Does this variety of lines lead to discord or confusion?

2. Find examples of suggestions of line in nature, such as veins in a leaf, grain of wood, or branches of a tree.

(a) Can you find an example in nature where exact repetition is evident?

(b) Can you find an example of variety that does not lead to unity?

3. Collect examples of actual materials that have a linear quality—paper clips, string, yarn, bamboo, matches, toothpicks, wire, etc.

The following experiments may help you to create your own designs with special emphasis on the element of line.

1. Make an assortment of kinds of lines—straight, curved, zigzag,

77

wavy—with various tools such as pencil, pen, brush, crayon, chalk, tongue depressors, cord.

The photographs of designs shown in this chapter and others should not be expected to serve as models, but more as suggestions of the possibilities and limitations of particular tools and materials.

2. Move your hands in the air in a line pattern inspired by the rhythm of music. When you have a feeling for the rhythm, use chalk and develop a border design on paper. See Figs. 3-28 and 3-29 for examples of a rhythmical border and allover pattern developed from the sound of an African drum beat. They were made with paint and cut paper. The timing of the beats and the tone quality of the musical sounds will automatically suggest to each individual a different arrangement of lines.

3. Work with tools in many ways—freehand, with a ruler, or using different amounts of pressure on the tool. A brush was used with varying amounts of pressure to produce different thicknesses of lines. Basically parallel, or continuous and overlapping lines, curved or relatively straight and angular lines produce continuous borders or repeats for all-over patterns. Some of the lines are dark because of the amount of paint in the brush, whereas others give a "dry-brush" effect. In Fig. 3-48 and 3-49 a felt pen was held flat for some lines and on edge for other lines. Even the overlapping of lines creates the optical illusion of interlacing.

4. Work with ink and paint in a variety of techniques on dry, damp, rough, and smooth backgrounds; crumpled paper, wax crayon resist, and scratch board. As in Fig. 3-50, rubber cement dripped on a white or colored background and then covered with India ink can produce a rhythmical line design if the rubber cement is thin enough to drip in a satisfactorily thick and thin manner. When dry the rubber cement can be

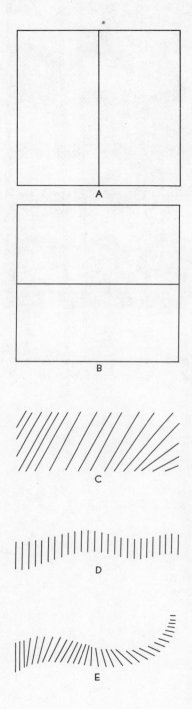

Fig. 3-46   To create optical illusions: A, the vertical line tends to carry the eye up and down and lengthen the shape; B, the horizontal line tends to carry the eye across the figure and broaden the shape; C, the diagonal lines tend to make the right end appear to be wider; D, the straight lines emphasize the rhythm of a contour shape, such as a fence; E, the straight lines create the illusion of the fence standing up at the left and lying down at the right end.

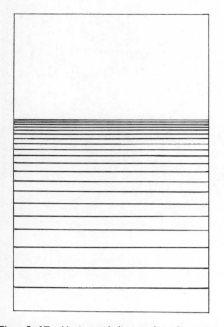

Fig. 3-47 Horizontal lines placed progessively closer together as they reach an horizon line give the effect of distance.

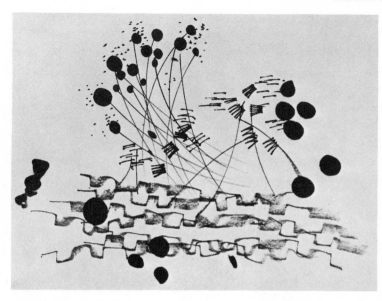

Fig. 3-48 Shaded and thin-sharp lines are made with a felt pen, with ink spots for variation in dark and light.

Fig. 3-49 Lines made with a felt pen held flat for the solid lines and held on edge for the double lines. Lines were overlapped to create the optical illusion of interlacing.

rubbed off to reveal the line design. Sometimes additional lines can be scratched through the remaining black of the background for added decorative effect. Ink on a wet background gives a fuzzy line effect. See Fig. 3-51.

Scratchboard, which is available in most school supply stores, can be covered with India ink. This gives a satisfactory surface on which to scratch lines freehand as in Fig. 3-52 or along a ruler as in Fig. 3-53. See Figs. 3-54 through 3-60 for other examples of line designs.

5. Make a border or all-over pattern with materials such as yarn, toothpicks, paper clips, or cut paper strips.

Fig. 3-50 Rubber cement dripped on a light background and then covered with India ink. When dry, the rubber cement was rubbed off to reveal the white lines.

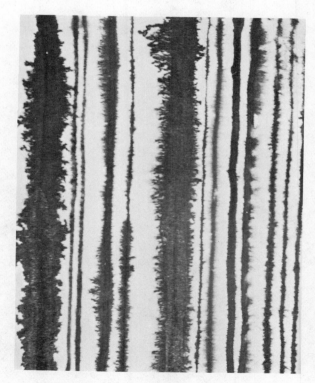

Fig. 3-51 India ink lines on a wet background spread slightly and give a decorative fuzzy line. (Student design.)

Fig. 3-52 India ink is painted over a piece of "scratch board." Freehand lines in graceful curves are scratched through the ink.

80

Fig. 3-53 Another India ink and scratch board technique, using all straight lines scratched along a ruler.

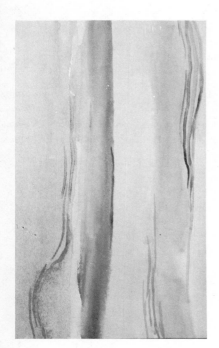

Fig. 3-54 Soft, irregular, broad lines of related values give an effective background for groups of narrow, uneven lines. (Student design.)

Fig. 3-55 Jagged lines may be made with a shaky hand motion in holding the brush. (Student design.)

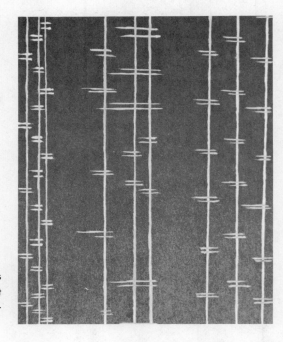

Fig. 3-56 Groups of thin lines placed at varying distances apart provide unity with variety. (Student design.)

Fig. 3-57 A wet background, horizontal swatches of paint, and the paper held in a vertical position allows the paint to drip downward in an irregular linear pattern. (Student design.)

6. Think of words that could be expressed with line—anger, sadness, boldness, daintiness. Select a tool and a medium which you think would best express each word and create a pattern of lines. Try combining dainty with bold, angry with happy, to determine what factors are involved in using these combinations harmoniously together.

7. Art education students might like to imagine a story they could tell to a group of young children in experimenting with line. Have the children express with kinds and qualities of lines the incidents in the story.

Young Johnny started home from school. Many things interested him along the way. He skipped merrily along until he came to a field of daisies. He stopped to wander among them and pick a bouquet. A bee buzzed among them. He darted from the bee. Then he leisurely wandered over to a brook. He stood along the bank throwing pebbles into the water and watching the rings spread out. Tiring of that, he slipped over to Mr. Robinson's pasture; but the bull spied him and lumbered towards him. Johnny ran as fast as his feet would carry him and crawled under the fence. He ran towards home,

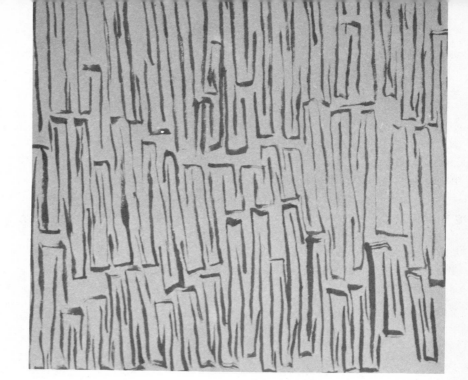

Fig. 3-58 Broken and continuous lines may suggest an irregular ''fret'' design. (Student design.)

Fig. 3-59 Purposeful curved lines of varying thickness produce a strong rhythm. (Student design.)

panting and all out of breath. Finally he sat down on the side of the road to rest a while. In the shade of the trees and on this beautiful sunny day, he fell asleep.

With each of the line experiments strive for new arrangements that are carefully planned but which give a quality of casual freedom. Imagine that the design is for an allover pattern for a placemat, for wallpaper, for a formica cabinet top, a shopping bag, gift-wrapping paper, or whatever idea may appeal to the imagination. Develop an appreciation of the element of line for *itself* rather than expecting it to be used to represent something with which you are already familiar, such as a flower or an animal. In the latter case, you think more of the *shape* you are producing than the kind or quality of *line*.

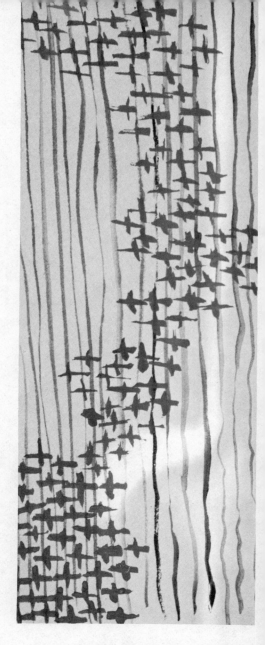

Fig. 3-60 Free-brush vertical lines may form a background for an irregular linear pattern of crosses. (Student design.)

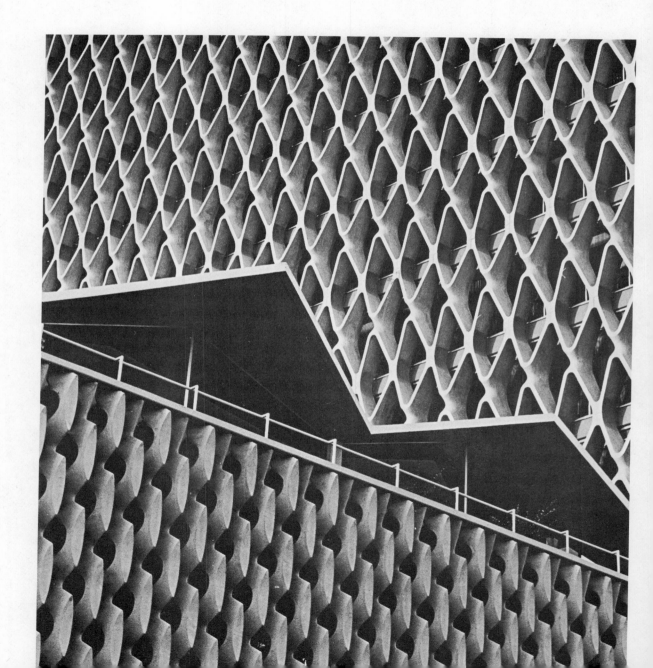

4

THE SHAPE OF THINGS

Extend a line around an area and what do you have?—a two-dimensional shape. Give this shape sides and a top and it becomes a three-dimensional form. In other words, *shape* may be viewed as a flat enclosure of space; *form* as volume surrounded by limiting factors. We may also be conscious of the areas outside and inside a shape or form. These are sometimes referred to as positive and negative areas or shapes. The actual shape or area within the contour is the positive while the area outside is the negative. Both must be considered in planning a basic design of any importance. When shapes are repeated or related ones used together, we refer to the arrangement as a pattern. Note the interesting patterns achieved by various building materials illustrated in Fig. 4-1. There will be further discussion of pattern at the end of this chapter.

STRUCTURAL DESIGN

We may be concerned with designing either a structural shape or a decorative one. The *structural* shape or form is that which is made by the length, width, depth, color, and texture of an area. It may be an actual shape, like a piece of paper, or a drawing of a shape on paper, or a

Fig. 4-1 Materials used for contemporary architectural purposes show a variety of shapes organized in exciting patterns. (Photograph by Don Murray.)

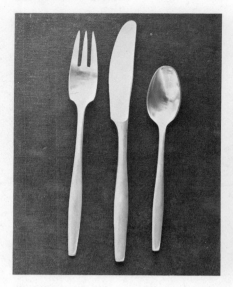
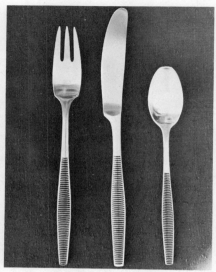

Fig. 4-2 The shapes of the stainless steel flatware express a quality of satisfactory structural design. They have character and beauty because of their fitness to their purpose. They have a frank simplicity of form, beautiful proportions, and the stainless steel is a material suited to both the purpose and the manufacturing process. (Variation #V, courtesy of Dansk Designs, Inc., Great Neck, New York.)

Fig. 4-3 The structural shape of the stainless steel flatware is simple and beautiful in proportion, as well as functional. However, to satisfy some individual tastes, a decorative design which is simple and subordinated to the shape, actually adding emphasis to the structural form, has been added. (Variation #VI, courtesy of Dansk Designs, Inc., Great Neck, New York.)

three-dimensional model. A *decorative shape* is one that is used as surface enrichment of the structural design. In designing the structural shape or form we are concerned mainly with the following problems:

1. Is it beautifully proportioned?
2. Is it suited to its purpose?
3. Is it suited to the materials and processes which will be followed in making it?
4. Does it express individuality and creative thinking?

Reread, in Chapter 2 the material concerning the principle of proportion. In Fig. 4-2, consider the quality of simplicity and graceful proportions that have been incorporated into the lines of the stainless steel flatware. The tines of the fork are shorter and further apart than those in the older designs. Thus they are easier to clean. The handle and the blade of the knife are both molded as one because the whole piece is made of stainless steel—not just the blade as in silver flatware. The curves of the handles fit the hand comfortably.

Let us assume we are designing a rectangular shape to be used basically as a living room. It might be made 15′ × 18′. Or if it is to be

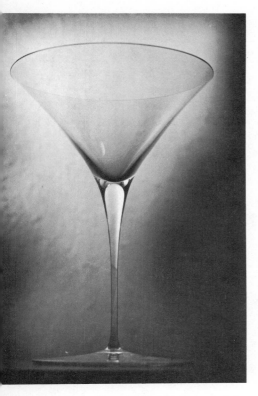

Fig. 4-4 The very delicate long stem of the hand-blown cocktail glass of Lobmeyr crystal is a structural shape that would grace the most formal table. "Ambassador" pattern, Lobmeyr crystal. (Photograph courtesy of J. and L. Lobmeyr, Vienna Austria. Designed by Professor Oswald Haendtl of the Vienna Academy for Applied Arts, 1934.)

Fig. 4-5 The short-stemmed sherbet of the Royal Leerdam crystal has a sturdy, informal appearance. "Tango" pattern in Royal Leerdam. (Photograph courtesy of A. J. Van Dugteren and Sons, Inc.)

used for a combination living and dining area, 15′ × 21′ might be a better proportion. As far as pleasing proportions are concerned, each shape might be equally satisfactory, but to suit the functions for which it will be used, the shape must be varied accordingly.

If a design is to become a piece of tableware made from glass, one would wish to know whether it was to be used every day or for special occasions. Delicate handblown glass, such as that in "Ambassador" pattern in Lobmeyr crystal becomes even more delicate when designed with a long stem for more formal use (see Fig. 4-4). Relatively heavy glass such as the "Tango" pattern in Royal Leerdam crystal is quite appropriate in a short-stemmed design for informal use (see Fig. 4-5). Both are designed from the standpoint of a beautiful, unadorned structural form for the particular use for which it was intended.

The purpose for which we are planning to use the form will determine to a large extent the proper evaluation of it. It might be unsatisfactory for one purpose, but be very fine for another use. *Our* tastes will naturally enter into our evaluation of a "good form" for a particular function. If we can learn to select a design in a broadminded manner and apply the principles of design, the resulting choice of the organization of the elements will usually be a happy solution of the problem. We may need to make many trial arrangements of the elements in order to finally choose the most satisfactory one. This is by no means a waste of time, however, for by this method we develop skill, a better sense of discrimination, and may eventually arrive at a technique of working that may be characterized as distinctly our own. This is what most artists are striving for.

Lines within the material, such as the grain in wood, may suggest to the artist the form of the object that can be made from it. The curve of a grain line may suggest the upward swing of an arm for the sculpture of a figure. The series of irregular curves may remind him of the folds of drapery in a skirt. If we are constantly aware of the many characteristics in materials we shall find that we will continually design with them in mind. We will not force the material to do what it does not wish to do. We will let it work for us and with us.

The tools and processes or techniques used in making an object will definitely alter its form. In making a piece of wood sculpture, if one has only a knife to whittle with, the size of the form may be small. If one has a power saw, he may use a large piece of wood and take off large areas of wood which he does not want for the final design. These pieces, in turn, may give inspiration for other designs that can be made from them. But if one has only carving tools, the extra wood must be cut off in small gouges, thus becoming wood shavings that may or may not be usable for other designs. Note the wooden candle holders in Fig. 4-6. Measure with your eyes the variation in spacing between the top and the narrow part (or neck), between the neck and the sweeping lines of the base. Neither space is exactly one-third or one-fourth of the others, thus giving a pleasing subtleness to the proportions. Note the variation of heights in the tops of the two candle holders. Just this little change from the ordinary expresses sufficient individuality and creative thinking on the part of the designer.

In this text we are mainly concerned with suggestions for creating designs for decorative purposes. However, in most chapters, the emphasis is also on certain factors that need to be considered in the development and/or appreciation of good structural shapes or forms. You must have a structural shape of some kind—even a two-dimensional one—before you can add the decorative design. We would hope that the space within which one plans a decorative design would be considered the structural shape and plan it as carefully as the lines and shapes within the space. Is the structural shape to be tall and slender, broad and bulky, squarish, a round or oval shape? Is it a natural form, a simple geometric shape, or an irregular shape? Whatever the structural design one plans, we should not think of it just as a means to an end, but as a definite,

Fig. 4-6 The design of the beautiful wooden candle holders fulfills all the requirements of a satisfactory structural design.

Fig. 4-7 The designer of the glass ashtray has made use of variation in thickness and height for a more pleasing structural design. (Photograph by Randy Miller.)

important part of the whole design, whether it stops with only the structural design, or goes one step further and has a decorative design applied.

Note the structural design of the glass ashtray illustrated in Fig. 4-7. Although it is basically a round shape, the thickness of the glass has been varied and the height of one side is greater than the other. Besides using it as an ashtray, the imaginative person might also use it as a small flower container, a candy dish, or just a beautiful accessory on a table top.

The structural design may have a "decorative character" due to the unusualness of the functional form, as in the ashtray or the candle holders discussed previously. The material from which the object is made may have a decorative effect that is a part of that particular material, such as the grain in wood, or the texture of a fabric or a stone. Innumerable objects in nature have beautiful patterns that have *grown* as a part of the development of that particular object. Note the characteristic patterns of spots and bumps that have grown in a definite organization of texture on the surface of the shells shown in Figs. 4-8, 4-9, and 4-10. Note the pattern of dark and light on the head and around the neck of the cat shown in Fig. 4-11. (Compare this natural pattern with the decorative geometric pattern on the man-made abstract cats shown in Figs. 4-16c and

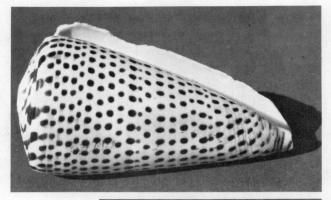

Fig. 4-8 A shell that has a polka-dot pattern which has developed as a part of the structure has an entirely different character when viewed from the large coiled end.

Fig. 4-9 End of the shell shown in Fig. 4-8.

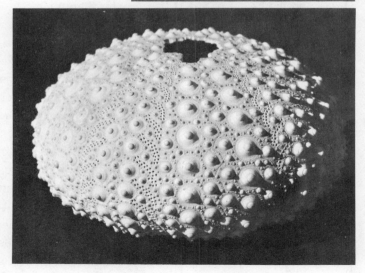

Fig. 4-10 A shell picked up along the beach expresses a decorative quality in the structural form because of the pattern of "bumps" throughout its surface.

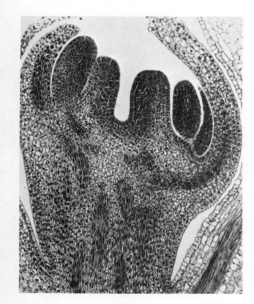

Fig. 4-11 The fur and hairs of animals often develop a natural pattern in the variety of colors. "Henry" is very proud of his striped collar and facial pattern. (Owned by Letta Lockhart.)

Fig. 4-12 A photomicrograph of the transverse section of a lily anther. Note the natural pattern of the cellular structure. (Photograph courtesy of Dr. Earl D. Camp, Chairman, Dept. of Biology, Texas Technological College.)

4-30.) Recall the pattern of stripes in a zebra's coat, the dots of color on a butterfly's wings, the beautiful plummage of hundreds of varieties of birds. These are all natural patterns that may serve as inspirations for our man-made decorative designs. Note the composition of pollen grains in the photomicrograph of the transverse section of a lily anther, as shown in Fig. 4-12. Anyone interested in creative stitchery could get much inspiration from this.

DECORATIVE DESIGN

A *decorative design* is one which is the surface enrichment of the structural shape or form. By "surface enrichment" we mean the applied decoration, such as a printed or painted design, one that is etched, carved, appliqued, or otherwise executed to decorate the surface of an area. In creating the decorative design we are concerned with those same four problems as in structural design, plus the following additional ones:

1. Does the decoration strengthen the shape of the object by emphasizing or harmonizing with its proportions?
2. Is the decoration used in moderation?
3. Does the decoration reinforce the function?

In planning the surface enrichment many terms may be used to classify the shapes found in the design, such as:

1. Realistic
2. Abstract
3. Nonobjective

   (a) Geometric
   (b) Free form or biomorphic.

REALISTIC DESIGNS

We have often heard or read the old cliché that there is no place in art today for the artist who represents objects in a realistic manner because the camera can do his work so much better. We have also become familiar with the repeated criticism of nonobjective art: "My five-year old son could do as well." As a rebuttal to those ideas, let us think for a bit about the many areas of art in which precise accuracy in representation of a shape is most necessary—even today! What architect strives to show his sketches of his buildings in any except their true form? What industrial designer will find it to his advantage to abstract a shape? He may be employed to improve a product by changing its proportions or its mechanics of operation, but the sketches or the models that he makes are as near the final proportions of the actual product as he is capable of making them. In some commercial catalogs, it may not be practical to use photographs, so the artist makes renderings to represent actual objects advertised in the catalogs, which he portrays in a very realistic manner. The artist might portray specific details or eliminate others so much more efficiently than a camera would do in a similar job. In Fig. 4-13 the architect's rendering of the building is done in a relatively realistic manner, whereas the people and trees and shrubbery are abstract.

Most professional artists who work in an abstract or nonobjective manner have been trained in realistic representation in early classes in freehand drawing. When they are thoroughly aware of every detail of the realistic form, *then* they can let their imaginations soar to higher levels of creative thinking. That road may lead them in paths of childlike simplicity of shape, as in the paintings by Miro, see Fig. 4-14, or to a more

Fig. 4-13 The rendering of a proposed building which an architect plans for a client must be sufficiently accurate in detail for the client to be able to visualize the actual building of the future. But the architect also depicts the shrubbery, trees, and people in a simple, abstract manner to add decorative touches to his rendering. (Architect's rendering of the Branch Facilities of the First Federal Savings and Loan Association, Lubbock, Texas. Schmidt and Stuart, A.I.A., Architects and Engineers.)

complicated form of abstraction as in Picasso's "Three Musicians" (see Fig. 4-15). Whatever the final design may be, if it is a true work of art, it represents a varied background of training from realistic to nonobjective representation.

What we so often refer to as realistic or representational shapes are those which represent flowers, birds, fish, landscapes, etc., in an easily recognizable form. The petals on the rose curl back and show the drops of dew; the texture appears as soft velvet. Most realistic designs have little merit for *decorative* purposes. Many people could recognize the confusion that would result from placing meat and potatoes on a flower-bedecked plate. A feeling of uneasy comfort may result from walking on a floral designed carpet. A scenic wallpaper seldom has more than passing ap-

Fig. 4-14 Composition, 1933, by Joan Miro expresses a childlike simplicity of shape. [Gift of the Advisory Committee (by exchange). Collection The Museum of Modern Art.]

peal. A realistic sculpture of a noted person will often find its way into a dusty corner of a public building because of its mediocrity.

A true work of art needs more than an exact likeness to something from nature for it to have lasting appeal. It is quite possible the artist can give the design more character by introducing an unusual color combination or use a rendering technique that arouses the curiosity of passersby. This, of course, is like portraying the "Boy with Green Hair" which immediately takes it out of the realm of the truly realistic. But as far as the element of shape is concerned, it could be as near the natural form as the artist could portray. He uses other elements, such as color and texture, to give it surprise and lasting beauty.

Note the wood carvings in Figs. 4-16a, b, and c. In (a) a realistic inter-

Fig. 4-15 *Three Musicians,* 1921, by Pablo Picasso expresses a more complicated form of abstraction. (Collection The Museum of Modern Art.)

97

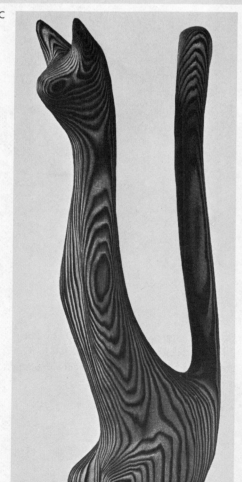

pretation of a dog represents skill in carving; but very little imagination has been shown, except in the use of the carving tool for a decorative effect. In (b) the carving of a pig shows a more simplified abstract design with more imagination shown in the carving and sanding. In (c) a more abstract carving of a cat is shown using the grain of the wood in an imaginative way as a decorative feature.

ABSTRACT

The *abstract* shape may draw its inspiration from nature, but it is definitely man-created. He has modified and organized the subject matter to make it suit the purpose for which he is going to use the design. He makes it express certain qualities such as dignity, gaiety, or grotesque-

Fig. 4-16 *A, A realistic interpretation of a dog represents skill in carving, but very little imagination has been shown except in the use of the carving tool for a decorative effect. B, The carving of a pig shows a more simplified abstract design with more imagination shown in the carving and sanding. C, A more abstract carving of a cat utilizing the grain of the wood for a decorative effect. (Photographs by Randy Miller.)*

ness. He may *simplify, exaggerate, rearrange,* and in general make a planned organization that involves the expression of his imagination. It may be a flat design, or it may express depth. In the majority of instances when a design is to be enjoyed for pure pleasure, the abstract shape will "live" longer. It may be a design on our china or crystal, a piece of sculpture, a painting, a dress fabric. If it is planned for lasting satisfaction, it will show a certain degree of abstraction. The *simplification* makes the design more easily understood or serves as a shorthand method of representation or symbolization. The *exaggeration* gives it more individuality. The *rearranging* brings the resulting attribute of harmony and fitness to purpose, tools, materials, and processes that will be followed in the completion of the design.

For *emotional* effects, a shape may be changed from its usual proportions to those that are more exaggerated or distorted. The early cross was designed with the horizontal bar about one-third the length of the vertical part. For deeper pull on the emotions look earnestly at the cross whose horizontal bar is about one-fifth the length of the vertical part. It draws the eyes upward and holds them in reverence as the designer had anticipated that it would.

The Oriental artist has long been noted for his ability to distort or exaggerate a part of a figure for the purpose of making it seem more important, whereas the less important was minimized by making it smaller than the usual proportions.

Any variation from the naturalistic shape is one which requires first, the use of the imagination to visualize, and second, the ability to execute the vision into a satisfactory abstract form. Nature provides a wide variety of shapes for us to see and enjoy, but these are only a few compared to the limitless variety that would be possible for the human mind to create from its own imagination. The more we use the imagination, the more active it becomes. The more we resort to copying the ideas of others, the more difficult it becomes to use our own imaginations.

In Fig. 4-17a the lowly pecan is shown in a photograph to give inspiration for the simple, abstract designs shown in b, c, and d. In Fig. 4-18 the pumpkin has been presented in a technique similar to "pointilism" to create a textured effect. In 4-19 the pumpkin has been cut into sections and reassembled in an exaggerated pattern of dark and light.

A

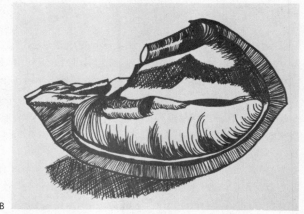

B

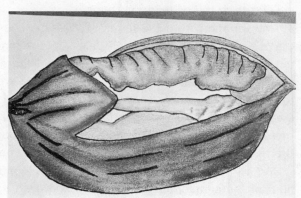

C

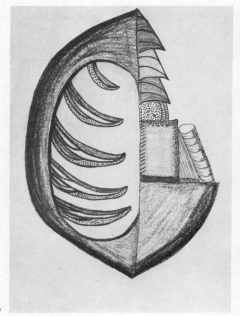

D

Fig. 4-17 The development of an abstract design may go through several stages before it reaches the most abstract form. (Photograph by Randy Miller.) *A,* photograph of the natural form of a pecan with a broken shell, *B, simplified* pen and ink representation, *C,* simplified abstract watercolor *suggesting* the pecan, *D,* chalk and pen sketch to *represent* the natural form.

Fig. 4-18 Simplified abstract design inspired from a pumpkin. Mosaic cut-paper collage. (Student design.)

Fig. 4-19 Simplified abstract design inspired from a pumpkin, using large areas of cut paper. (Student design.)

By studying each of these illustrations one can easily see the possible steps through which one might progress in the planning of an abstract design.

1. There is search for a possible subject to abstract. In most instances, the best choice is an object that expresses sufficient variation in organization to stimulate one's imagination to see possibilities for different ideas for designs that could be developed from it.

2. We need to study the subject thoroughly; sketch it in a variety of views; try different media and techniques of representation.

3. As we are making these sketches of the whole object or any part of it, we need to start simplifying, rearranging, and exaggerating the proportions in different areas in order to develop the final abstract design that will fit the size, shape, and function desired.

4. We need to experiment with different color combinations for the individual design, or ways of repeating the motif for a pattern. More will be discussed later in this chapter concerning the development of an allover repeat.

NONOBJECTIVE

GEOMETRIC SHAPES

A shape that we do not associate with anything from nature, such as saying it resembles a bird, a flower, etc., may be a mathematically precise shape such as a square, rectangle, triangle, circle, parallelogram, cube, or cylinder. These shapes are often thought of as having a dynamic quality. This beauty is derived from either elegance of proportions or their arrangement in relation to other shapes in a composition. Alexander Girard, in his fabric designs, has used simple geometric shapes of the simplest type—squares and circles—and yet his spacing, his colors and variations in dark and light lend a note of excitement and interesting variety to each new design.

Geometric shapes such as squares and rectangles have one quality in common, that of stability, because of their flat bases. Circles, ovals, spheres, and ellipses, however, have no true bases and seem to be, on the one hand, unstable and more capable of movement and, on the other hand, to possess a "built-in" quality of equilibrium.

In planning a geometric design there is sometimes the temptation to space the shapes in a very regular manner, mechanically measured and very regimental in character. The student of design must learn to develop a "feeling" for subtle irregularities of spacing, sizes of shapes, variation of dark and light color. Instead of expecting that each design must be made according to set rules, his designs will acquire the delightful unexpectedness which makes art what it is.

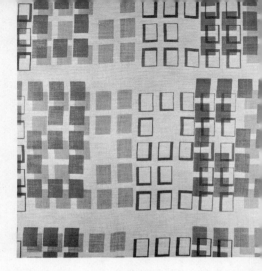

Fig. 4-20 Solid and linear rectangles, arranged in an overlapping pattern for an allover repeat. ("Geometrics," designed by Ethel Jane Beitler.)

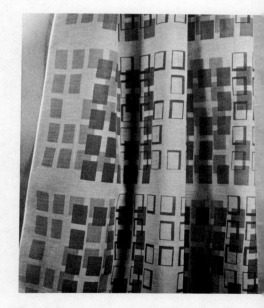

Fig. 4-21 For an allover fabric design that will hang in folds, the design must not only look well flat, but be enhanced by overlapping folds. ("Geometrics," designed by Ethel Jane Beitler.)

Fig. 4-22 Simple equilateral triangles may form hexagons and diamonds when combined in an allover pattern. The irregularity of dark, and light triangles lends added beauty to the pattern when it hangs in folds. ("Triangles," designed by Alexander Girard for the Herman Miller Furniture Company.)

Fig. 4-23 Large triangles and small squares form an interesting background pattern for the simple Christmas card design.

The fabric design in Figs. 4-20 and 4-21 has made use of solid and linear rectangles arranged in an overlapping pattern for an allover repeat. The overlapping gives the pattern depth. Common shapes like the equilateral triangle may be organized in an uncommon manner with pleasing irregularity of dark and light (see Fig. 4-22).

Note the interesting background in the simple Christmas card design in Fig. 4-23. The geometric shapes might suggest trees to the imaginative viewer with showers of tiny squares representing snowflakes. In Fig. 4-24 another arrangement of geometric shapes also suggests trees, while the metal scraps in geometric shapes in Fig. 4-25 were welded together to represent birds. In referring to these particular designs, we wish to suggest to the student that the designs are composed of geometric shapes, but have been developed into what one might also refer to as "abstract" designs because they suggest subject matter from nature.

It is very easy to make the suggestion of a form out of a flat geometric shape by the addition of shading. For instance, note the curved geometric shapes in Fig. 4-26. In Fig. 4-27 shading has been added to express light and shadow and the forms become rounded with substance and new meaning. They seem three-dimensional and give the suggestion that they may be viewed from all angles. The flat two-dimensional shapes with straight sides shown in Fig. 4-28 also become forms when other sides are added besides the shading, as in Fig. 4-29. Although this change from a flat two-dimensional shape into a three-dimensional form has been illus-

103

trated with geometric designs, it also applies, of course, to all other types of designs: namely, realistic, abstract, or nonobjective.

IRREGULAR AND BIOMORPHIC SHAPES

Frequently we may start out with a basically geometric shape and gradually change it to a free, irregular one. We may round the corners of a square, or dip in the sides in an irregular manner, making it a less precise but more intriguing shape. We may go further and open the shape in the center or cut into the side in an irregular manner. These shapes suggest to us the biomorphic shapes so frequently found in nature. The bean is basically a triangle with rounded corners. The apple is a circle with a dimple!

In Fig. 4-31 similar irregular shapes are organized for a serigraph. They seem to have been suggested by a pattern of cut slabs of stone.

Fig. 4-24 Triangles of various sizes and shapes are grouped together to suggest tall, stately "trees."

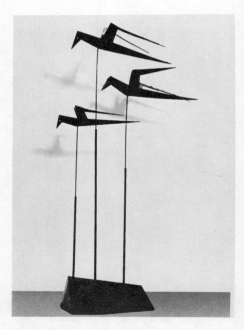

Fig. 4-25 Metal sculpture representing abstract bird forms constructed of basically geometric shapes. ("Leaving the Nest," designed by Bill Lockhart.)

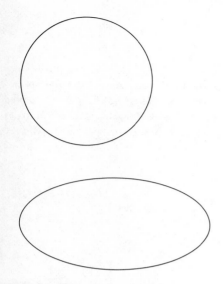

Fig. 4-27 Flat two-dimensional shapes become "forms" when shading is added.

Fig. 4-26 Flat two-dimensional shapes.

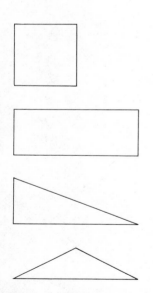

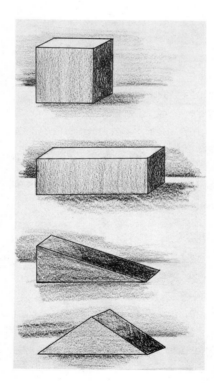

Fig. 4-28 Flat two-dimensional shapes with straight sides.

Fig. 4-29 When other sides are added, the "shapes" become "forms" and three dimensional.

Fig. 4-30 The structural form of the ceramic cat has been simplified and distorted in proportions from the natural form and decorated with a geometric design of squares and circles as a part of the clay body. (Photograph by Randy Miller.)

In Fig. 4-32 compare the three irregular shapes. The first one has been made from a shape which was basically a triangle, but the angles were rounded and the sides curved inward. This takes away from the precise angularity and the measured accuracy of the triangle. In the second shape a few deeply curved notches have been cut into the long side, but note that these notches, for more pleasing proportions, vary in size and are not cut right in the center of the side. In the third shape the center has been cut away in an irregular manner, making the sides of the broad angle relatively thick, whereas the long side is thin and has a break in it off-center.

In Fig. 4-33 a variety of irregular shapes harmonize with each other and fit together almost like a jig-saw puzzle.

The fact that shapes are related not only make them harmonize with each other more satisfactorily for a design, but it may also give the design added meaning and character. Compare the shapes in Figs. 4-31 and 33. The shapes in Fig. 4-31 express harshness because of the sharp angles, whereas the shapes in Fig. 4-33 express softness because of the graceful curves.

ALLOVER PATTERNS

The ability to plan a single unit for an abstract or nonobjective design is not a simple problem if one considers all the factors such as: design inspiration, organization according to the principles of design, and the purpose for which the design is to be used, as well as the technique, tools,

106

Fig. 4-31 Irregular shapes which might have been suggested by a pattern of cut slabs of stone. (Serigraph, "Fossilforms," by Dean Meeker, photograph courtesy of Quepha Rawls, owner.)

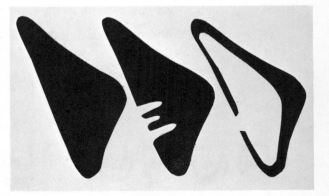

Fig. 4-32 Irregular shapes may be made more interesting sometimes by cutting into the side or making an open or hollow shape.

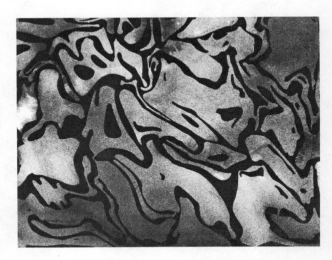

Fig. 4-33 Shadow patterns, or oil on water sometimes suggest a pattern of irregular shapes such as this one.

107

and media. Add these factors to the problem of repeating the single unit for an allover pattern.

What are some of the many ways in which an allover pattern may be developed? (see diagrams in Fig. 4-34 *a* through *l.*)

1. We may use identical motifs and arrange them:

    (a) Next to each other both horizontally and vertically.
    (b) In a half-drop position.
    (c) In a quarter-drop position.
    (d) In a checkerboard.
    (e) In a diamond effect.

Fig. 4-34 *A,* simple horizontal and vertical repeat; *B,* half-drop repeat; *C,* quarter-drop repeat; *D,* checkerboard repeat; *E,* diamond repeat; *F,* simple repeat, space between varied.

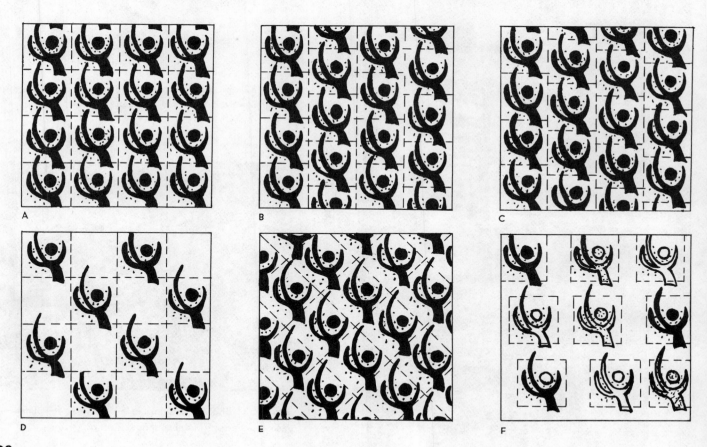

(f) At intervals, with varying space between.

(g) With alternation of position—upside down, or flipped over to the right to give a bisymmetrical appearance.

(h) By using reverse values of dark and light in alternate shapes.

(i) By changing the direction.

(j) By using the same basic shape, but varying the size.

(k) By overlapping for a suggestion of various planes.

(l) By using an "ogee" curve in an alternate repeat.

2. We may use different shapes in the same patterns as suggested above, but keep a feeling of unity by using related shapes to tie the whole design together. Units that are too widely spaced or combine too many

Fig. 4-34 *G, alternation of position; H, reverse value repeat; I, "French Repeat"—five directions; J, varied sizes, same motif; K, overlapped motifs to suggest different planes; L, "Ogee" curve repeat.*

varieties of shapes give a nonunified or confusing effect. We might refer to the different design units by number and combine them in a definite sequence, as 1, 1, 2, 1, 1, 2. See Fig. 4-37 for an example of a more complicated sequence arrangement.

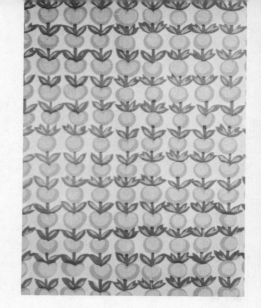

The photographs of the allover patterns illustrate a few of the arrangements indicated in the diagrams in Fig. 4-34 plus other more complicated methods of repeating the units.

Fig. 4-35 illustrates the most basic type of repeat, as shown in diagram (a) in Fig. 4-34a. For relief from monotony, the cherries and leaves are varied just a tiny bit in size and shape. The pattern in Fig. 4-36 is also, like the cherry motif, a basic repeat of all the same unit in the same size, with variation introduced in the hues and values.

Our first glance at the pattern shown in Fig. 4-37 would seem to suggest a similar basic repeat as that in the flower pattern, except with the use of three separate units. However, the variation of dark and light and the placement of the motifs shows a sequence that one could indicate as follows: starting at the top left corner with the large dark leaf as number 1 and reading across to the right, the sequence would be, 1, 2, 3, 1, 4, 5, 2, 6, 5, 2, 6, 5. For the vertical arrangement, the 1 and 4 always alternate, as do the 3 and 6. The 2's are always in the same column and so are the 4's.

Fig. 4-35 ''Manzanas,'' a basic horizontal and vertical allover repeat pattern. (Photo, courtesy of David and Dash Fabrics.)

In Fig. 4-38 the lines at the edge of the photograph indicate the beginning and ending of the repeat. There is great variety in size and placement and yet all of the shapes are unified because of the general circular character of the units which are combined.

In Fig. 4-40 the typical ''ogee'' pattern has been used for an upholstery fabric. Variety has been achieved through the combination of different values in an irregular manner. The dark lines at the edge of the photograph indicate the moderately short repeat.

Fig. 4-41 shows a typical half-drop or hexagon effect by placing one unit half way between the two in the row above. The design is planned so the ones in the second row can fit between the two in the first row in the half-drop. A variation of the half-drop is shown in Fig. 4-42. Alternation of units in an upside down position also add interest to the repeat. In Fig. 4-43 the motifs in the second row are placed between the ones

Fig. 4-38 #105, ''Duke,'' a variable allover repeat pattern which is unified by the size and shape of the curved units. (Photograph courtesy of Wesco Fabrics, Inc.)

Fig. 4-36 "Quatrefoil," by Alexander Girard, a basic horizontal and vertical allover repeat with variation of hues. (Photograph courtesy of Herman Miller Furniture Co.)

Fig. 4-37 "Jessica," suggestion of a basic allover repeat, but with a variation in the values to add interest. (Photograph courtesy of David and Dash Fabrics.)

Fig. 4-39 #125 "Nu-Tone," an allover repeat pattern with a suggestion of a half-drop effect. (Photograph courtesy of Wesco Fabrics, Inc.)

Fig. 4-40 #3212, Matelasse, upholstery fabric with a typical "ogee" pattern. (Photograph courtesy of Westgate Fabrics, Inc.)

Fig. 4-41 "Elstra," shows a half-drop effect in a hexagon allover repeat pattern. (Photograph courtesy of David and Dash Fabrics.)

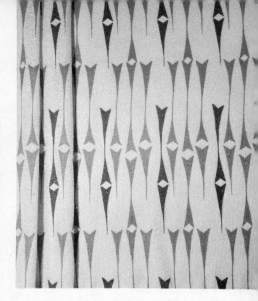

Fig. 4-42 "Mar Beta," a half-drop allover repeat pattern in which the units have been alternated in an upside-down position. (Photograph courtesy of Wesco Fabric, Inc.)

Fig. 4-43 The shapes in the second row are placed between two in the first row, but added interest is gained through overlapping of linear shapes to suggest different planes. (Designer, Miss Donna Read.)

in the first row, but additional interest is gained through the pattern of linear shapes which overlap and give a suggestion of different planes.

In Fig. 4-44 a vertical sequence of 1, 1, 2, 1, 1, 2 is suggested in the repeat in the vertical panel.

The reverse-cyma curve with variations in dark and light lend interest to the pattern illustrated in Fig. 4-45. The reverse curves give an illusion of folds on a flat fabric.

Turning a design in five different directions is a tricky method of making an interesting pattern. A similar way of changing the pattern in five directions is illustrated in diagram (*h*) in Fig. 4-34. Twenty-five squares may be arranged as the dotted lines indicate, and the motif placed in a different square in each of the five rows and turned in a different direction each time. Smaller motifs may be combined in some of the other squares to give a more compact design. This is sometimes referred to as a "French Repeat" (see Fig. 4-46).

A satisfactory allover pattern should be flat (two-dimensional), compact, and continuous in effect, so that we are more conscious of the allover pattern than of the individual units of which the pattern is composed.

Fig. 4-44 A vertical sequence of 1, 1, 2, 1, 1, 2 is suggested in the allover repeat. (Designer, Miss Donna Read.)

Fig. 4-45 A regular repeat of a suggested reverse cyma-curve with variations in dark and light. (C.-Pattern Right, Inc., a copyright design, photograph courtesy of Erbun Fabrics, Corporation.)

CREATIVE EXPERIMENTS

1. To develop an awareness of interesting shapes and forms:

    (a) Find examples of beautifully proportioned shapes and forms in nature: pebbles, leaves, driftwood, and any other natural forms.
    (b) Find illustrations of beautiful natural shapes and forms: pictures of trees, flowers, animals, birds, fish.
    (c) Find examples of exciting new shapes in actual objects or illustrations of man-made functional designs: a molded plastic or plywood chair, an automobile fin, a piece of tableware, a new collar shape, a beautiful bottle (other shapes too numerous to list). Only the imagination and one's sensitivity to pleasing pro-

113

Fig. 4-46 A "French repeat" showing the unit turned in five different directions. (Designer, Miss Donna Read.)

portions would be the limiting factors in one's ability to find these examples.

(d) Find illustrations or actual examples of abstract and nonobjective shapes and forms in fabrics, wallpaper, sculpture, paintings.

2. To experiment with creating structural shapes and forms:

(a) Use cut paper or draw several rectangles of varying sizes and shapes to compare their proportions.

(b) Use cut paper or draw several shapes appropriate for silhouettes of vases, tumblers, goblets, or other tableware.

(c) Use one of your line designs and interpret it in terms of shape.

(d) Cut several geometric shapes of varying sizes. Make irregular shapes out of them by rounding an occasional corner or dipping in the side.

(e) Plan a three-dimentional form that could be carved from wood or soap.

(f) Find a piece of scrap wood which is a beautiful form and finish it for a piece of nonobjective sculpture.

3. To experiment with creating decorative designs:

(a) If the student has saved all of his scraps of paper from the designs in 2 a, b, c, and d above, these may suggest abstract decorative designs which could be assembled to represent amusing birds, animals, fish, or human figures with decorative designs applied for interest.

(b) Cut flat structural shapes representing Christmas tree ornaments and decorate with line designs organized into a decorative design.

(c) Plan an allover pattern of repeated shapes for wallpaper or giftwrapping paper.

5

SPACE—ALL OR NOTHING

Space is *nothing* until an area of reference is established. To establish this area of reference, we need to enclose or limit the space surrounding the said area. We may plan a certain size enclosure, or let it be the edge of the canvas on which an artist is painting, or the walls of the room that we are furnishing, or the whole outdoors as far as one can see. Space is *all of the area* within the enclosure of the outer fringe of our vision.

SPATIAL ORGANIZATION

Spatial organization may be two- or three-dimensional in character. This organization represents an interrelationship of the whole area, whether the area is flat or three-dimensional. Spatial organization includes the design of the shapes, the textures, and the colors within the space in relation to the whole space. If we were planning the furnishings for a room, there would be many ways in which we could study the total space. Such ways might consist of the following:

1. The floor space and the relative amount of area that each piece of furniture would occupy.
2. Each wall space with its relative amount of area that various pieces

Fig. 5-1 The strong contrast of values of the objects in the foreground as compared with the closely related values of the background areas give the impression of more distance. (Los Angeles Freeway. Photograph by Don Murray.)

117

of furniture and accessories occupy when placed against the wall, plus any architectural features, such as windows and doors.

3. The ceiling space with its division, and with beams or lighting fixtures.

4. The smaller areas of space in open shelves and on table and desk tops.

Most of our cities today are examples of myriads of buildings, huddled together with very little planning of the whole spatial organization. The plans of the city remodelers of today call for expensive demolishing of buildings, clearing large areas for superhighways, shopping centers, parking areas, and housing projects. If the designers of the past could have foreseen the future and could have had the cooperation of the citizens in planning their "City of the Future," the space could have been organized in a much more beautiful and efficient manner, so that today we could go on and merely add to the building of the city without first tearing down the old.

TWO-DIMENSIONAL SPACE

Before one can thoroughly understand all the underlying principles with which one would be concerned in the total spatial organization, one must first begin with a study of simple two-dimensional space. Let us enclose a definite size area as in Fig. 5-2a. This enclosure has length and width. Within this enclosure we may place another shape which is defined by an outline as in diagram (b). Our eyes then become aware of the space surrounding the inner shape and also the space within that shape. As we add other shapes to the space, tensions are created, causing the eyes to move from one shape to another in the order of their importance. The closer together objects are grouped, the more conscious we are of the *shapes*. The further apart, the more conscious we are of *space*. Our decision to emphasize one element in preference to another might be due to the *utilitarian* or to the *aesthetic* characteristics of the design, or both.

Fig. 5-2 Diagrams of movement in two-dimensional space.

118

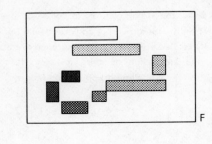

In diagrams (c) and (d) the movement in the space was created by means of contrast in the size and shapes. Movement might also be created by changing the directions of the shapes as in diagram (e).

Contrast of values in the shapes helps to intensify the feeling of movement in space, as in diagram (f).

The problems of placement of shapes in space involve all the principles of design, but more specifically the problem of proportion. In Chapter 2 in the discussion of this principle we made reference to the various ways in which space might be divided, employing repetition, variety, and a combination of repetition and variety. We suggest that the reader refer back to those paragraphs.

For purposes of helping the reader to become aware of the many ways in which the information in these chapters can be applied to various areas of life, let us apply to a room our discussion of the division of space. First, we must plan the floor space and locate the various pieces of furniture to scale. Correct planning of this kind will aid one in selecting the right scale of furniture and the correct number of pieces to fit the available space. A salesman might do a successful job of selling to a client a large desk, desk chair, credenza, lounge chair, and several guest chairs for his office. When his client has them delivered, however, he finds there is not room for all of them. If some preplanning had been done on paper first, the salesperson could have advised the client to select a smaller desk, credenza, and lounge chair. Or he could have left out the credenza and kept the large lounge chair. The diagram would also have indicated the amount of space available between the various pieces of furniture to allow for utilitarian as well as aesthetic needs. (See Figs. 5-3 and 5-4.)

A diagram of a wall area will allow the client to visualize architectural and decorative features which would need to be considered in relation to the furnishings. A high ceiling or a long wall space might be broken by strips of walnut to add color and distinction to the room. The diagram will also show the division of space. (See Fig. 5-5.)

The "open-stock" storage walls that are being produced today by a number of different manufacturing firms provide a challenge in selecting and organizing open and closed shelf space, drawer and filing space, provision for television, dictaphone, record player, and other equipment as the individual so desires. Most of the storage components are sus-

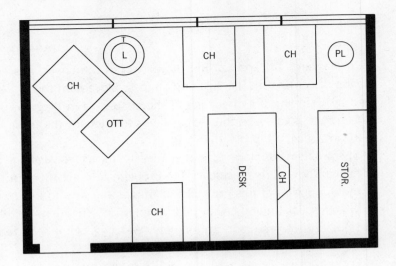

Fig. 5-3 The room is so crowded with furniture there is not sufficient space to move about comfortably.

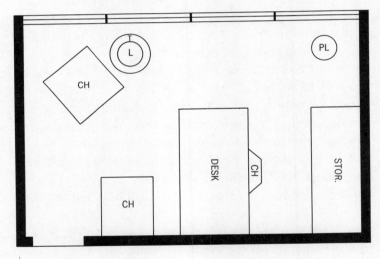

Fig. 5-4 By reducing the number of pieces of furniture, the room actually appears larger and is also much more convenient in arrangement.

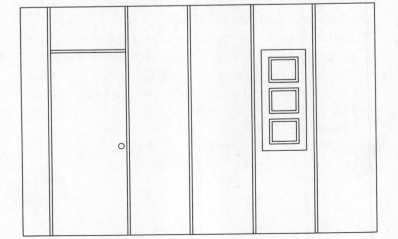

Fig. 5-5 The vertical divisions serve two purposes: (1) they might make the ceiling appear higher or (2) the length of the wall space might be made to appear shorter because the space is broken.

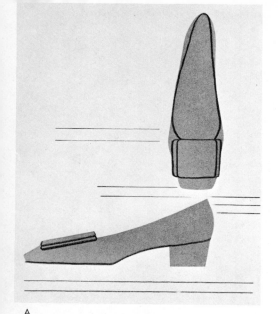

A

pended from the wall or from metal poles that span the space from floor to ceiling. The problem is one of breaking up the wall space in a pleasing and usable manner. Turn back to page 7, Fig. 1-3, to see the example of the Herman Miller Comprehensive Storage System as displayed in a show room as it might be organized for an office space or a home.

A commercial artist plans his division of space for a layout of an advertisement so that he can decide what area is going to have copy, what part will be devoted to illustration, and where the firm name will be placed. A number of quick thumbnail sketches will give him a variety of ideas for his space organization. (See Figs. 5-6a, b, c, and d).

THREE-DIMENSIONAL SPACE

The appearance of a third dimension, that of depth, may be evidenced in the placement of shapes within a space. Contrast of size intensifies the illusion of depth. In Fig. 5-7a, note that the shape appears to be in the foreground because it is relatively large and placed at the bottom of

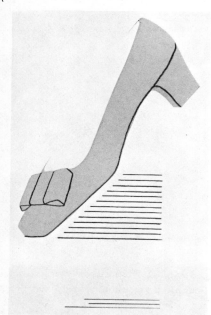

B

Fig. 5-6 Experiments with thumbnail sketches of layouts help one in arriving at a satisfactory arrangement of space. (Photograph by Randy Miller.)

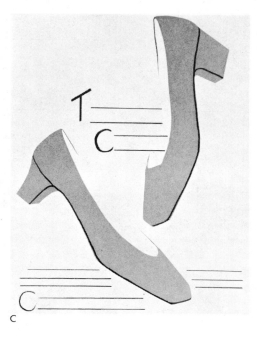

C

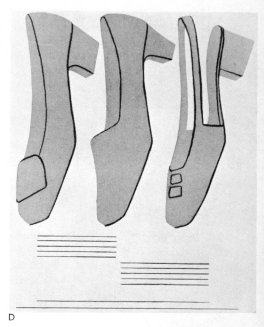

D

121

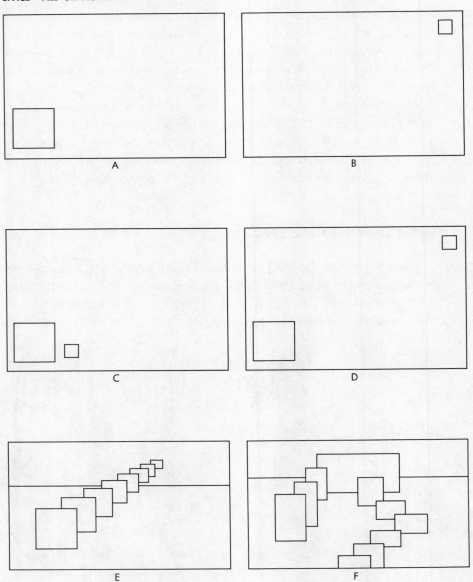

Fig. 5-7 Size and placement of objects within an enclosure suggest varying degrees of distance or movement in space.

Fig. 5-8 Space is represented by gradation of sizes and overlapping of shapes. (Photograph by Randy Miller.)

the space. In (b) the shape appears to be in the background, or far away, because it is relatively small and placed at the top of the space.

In diagram (c) the base of the shapes is on the same level, so that they appear to vary a great deal in size. In diagram (d) the optical illusion of depth is created.

In diagram (e) the feeling of distance is created by the gradual decrease in size of the square as it moves into the background, whereas in (f) the shapes not only move into the background but come back into the foreground again.

In the photograph of the row of Volkswagons (see Fig. 5-8), space is especially evident because of the apparent decrease of size as the vision extends in the distance. Also the overlapping of forms creates an effect of distance. Note in Fig. 5-9 how the distance is suggested by the progression of sizes of black spots, and the depth of the crater becomes greater toward the center of the group of small dots. In Fig. 5-10 the black shapes (positive spaces) have been organized to suggest cracked earth as the result of an earthquake. The groupings of tiny shapes give more depth to the crevasses and suggest the movement of the crack from one part of the area to another. Note also, how the white areas (negative spaces) give the interesting linear pattern of cracks in the earth in the design as a whole. See Fig. 5-12 for a similar design statement in reverse values.

In Fig. 5-11 the photograph of the underside of a mushroom cap shows the actual depth down into the center from which the stalk grows. The depth is accentuated by the thin layers of gills extending from the outer rim down into the center.

We may create the illusion of volume by means of the placement of planes in space, or we may keep the space open and "untrapped." In Fig. 5-13 the planes touch only at the base, but they seem to enclose the space; whereas in Fig. 5-14 the planes touch and bisect, but the space is not trapped or enclosed. In some fields of architecture the walls seem to enclose space in a compact way, whereas in others the glass walls cause the interior and exterior walls to blend together and suggest open space. In Fig. 5-15 note how the spaces become smaller and more "enclosed" as we approach the folds, or as the angles between the folds become sharper.

Earlier in this chapter there were three two-dimensional floor and wall plans to show the planning of space in a room (see Figs. 5-3, 5-4, and 5-5). At the same time a simple perspective drawing of the same room would more fully illustrate the three-dimensional space. In Fig. 5-16 three room alcoves of varying depths are indicated by means of one-point perspective. Note that all the diagonal lines lead to the vanishing point

(left)
Fig. 5-9 Distance is suggested by the gradual decrease in size of the black dots. Depth of the "crater" is suggested by the small dots. (Student design.)

(right)
Fig. 5-10 The "negative" areas of white suggest the cracks in earth after an earthquake. The small black shapes suggest the depth of the crevices. (Student design.)

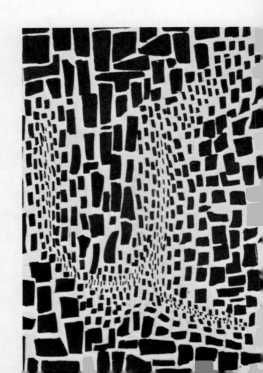

Fig. 5-11 The underside of a mushroom cap shows the depth down into the center from which the stalk grows. The depth is accentuated by the thin layers of gills extending from the rim down into the center. (Photograph by Randy Miller.)

Fig. 5-12 The opposite of Fig. 5-10. The white areas are the "positive areas" and the black linear pattern represents the "negative areas." (Student design.)

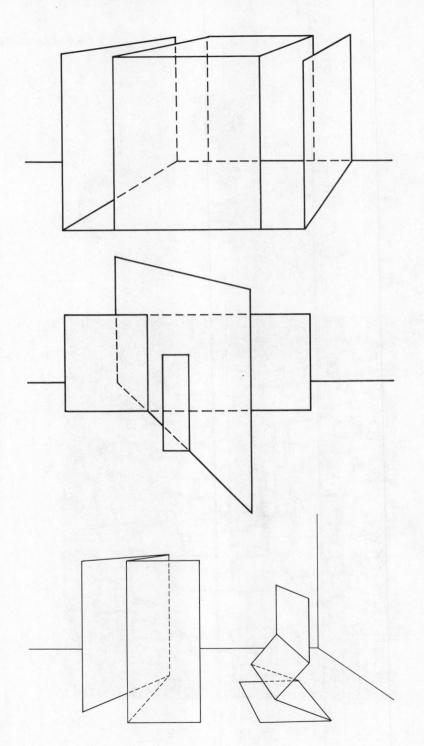

Fig. 5-13 Close to the vertical end pieces open areas have been left; thus the entire construction is an example of partially enclosed space.

Fig. 5-14 The planes placed at right angles do not enclose any area of space at any point.

Fig. 5-15 The spaces become smaller and more "enclosed" as we approach the folds, or as the angles between the folds become sharper.

126

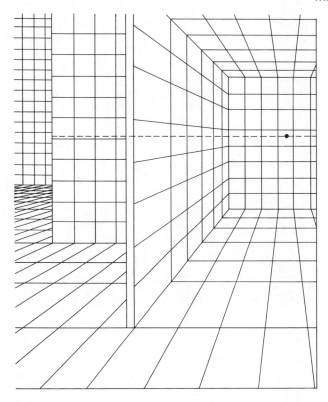

Fig. 5-16 One-point perspective suggesting three room alcoves of varying depths. All diagonal lines lead to the one vanishing point located close to the right-hand side of the composition.

located close to the right-hand side of the composition. The dotted line represents the eye level of the viewer. The horizontal and vertical lines become closer together as they move closer to the vanishing point.

Very frequently painters and commercial artists alter true perspective for the sake of emphasis. Painters will sometimes purposely indicate several sets of vanishing points within one picture in order to give a feeling of movement. Instead of presenting one static view to the viewer, the impression is given that the objects seen in the picture are being viewed from several vantage points. Advocates of the Cubistic form of expression take advantage of this form of representation of space from several viewpoints. Those who are interested in "Op Art" delight in creating unusual optical illusions of space by means of contrasts of dark and light or dramatic problems in perspective. Their statements of "movement in space" often leave one in a state of dizziness because of the violent

127

Fig. 5-17 Drawings of topographical maps showing hills and valleys by means of concentric rings to indicate the various elevations might inspire one for a rhythmical linear design expressing spatial heights. (Student design.)

actions created by the dark and light areas or the vibrations set up by the closely related values of strong intensities.

In Fig. 5-18 space has been suggested by the diminishing width of the street and the height of the buildings, but if you study the design carefully you will see that no attempt has been made to represent true perspective as in the diagram in Fig. 5-15. In Fig. 5-19 the composition is represented more as a child would visualize it. He knows the buildings in the foreground do not block his view of the ones across the street, so he made the buildings in the foreground smaller than the ones further away. He has suggested distance, however, by gradation of size of the buildings across the street. Distance can also be represented by a stark plainness, a lack of detail. In Fig. 5-20 the buildings are huddled together in the foreground, with the lonely expanse of land and the darkness of the night to remind one of the vast distance from other forms of civilization—closed in from everyone in the winter, and seldom seeing others in the summer.

In Fig. 5-21 space is emphasized by the placement and overlapping of figures. Also the doorway of the dwelling is in deep shadow, creating the effect of a deep space within. Also in Fig. 5-22 the contrasts of dark and

light express the expanse of space. In Fig. 5-1 the strong contrast of values shown in the overpass in the foreground as compared with the closely related values of the hills in the background gives the impression of distance.

SUMMARY OF WAYS OF CREATING THE ILLUSION OF DEPTH

More distance is expressed by:

A. Line

    1. Line movement from the foreground toward a vanishing point in the background.
    2. Broad lines in the foreground with thin ones in the background.

B. Shape

    1. Large shapes in the foreground with small ones in the background.

Fig. 5-18 The diminishing width of the street and sides of buildings suggests distance. (Student design.)

Fig. 5-19 Distance represented in a childlike manner. (Student design.)

Fig. 5-20 Distance represented by stark plainness of a lonely expanse of land. (Made by Mrs. Patricia Marlow.)

Fig. 5-21 Space is emphasized by the placement and overlapping of the figures. (Sculptured jewelry, "Dwelling," by Francis Stephen, Texas Tech University. Photograph by Randy Miller.)

Fig. 5-22 The blackness of the interior contrasts with the expanse of space seen beyond through the open doorway. (Photograph by Bill Crump.)

2. More detailed shapes in the foreground with less detail further away.

C. Color

1. Warm hues in the foreground with cooler ones in the background.
2. Strong contrasts of value up close with more closely related values to suggest distance.
3. Brighter intensities in the foreground with grayed forms in the background.

D. Texture

1. Sharpness of details in the foreground with fuzziness in the background.
2. Coarseness of textures in the foreground with more fineness further away.

CREATIVE EXPERIMENTS

1. To develop an awareness of space and ways that it can be expressed:

(a) Make a list of as many words as you can that would describe different kinds of space—actual, relative, inner, outer, surface, imaginative, aerial, infinite, hollow, two-dimensional, three-dimensional, moving, etc.

(b) Find examples in magazines that would illustrate some of the above words or others on your list.

(c) Find examples in magazines of:
(1) A "bird's-eye" view of space, as though you were in an airplane looking down on an area.
(2) A scene in which the objects in the foreground were bright and clear in color and those in the background were hazy, showing more distance.
(3) An artist's sketch using perspective to show distance from a vanishing point.

(d) Find examples of optical illusions which express impressions of space.

2. To experiment with creating examples of space and space division:

(a) Draw four rectangles which you consider are pleasing in proportion for enclosing space.

(b) Use all straight lines and divide the above rectangles into horizontal areas expressing:
(1) Gradation of size
(2) Repetition
(3) Variation
(4) Repetition and variation

(c) In a vertical rectangle, use shapes to express movement and distance (or a third-dimension).

(d) Make several tracings of (c) and experiment with dark and light values, and color to create different effects of distance.

(e) Use pieces of cardboard or balsa wood to experiment with examples of partially enclosed and open space, using at least three planes in each construction.

(f) Make a three-dimensional construction to be hung from the ceiling so it will move freely in space (a mobile).

6

COLOR SOUNDS OFF

Fig. 6-1 Any variation of values may be interpreted in any hue or intensity. (Photograph by Randy Miller.)

With our galaxy of colors in our homes, offices, factories, stores, our garments, our vehicles of transportation, it is difficult to imagine a world without color. Yet how many people go through life unaware of the beauty of color? But it has been only a generation ago, approximately, that our automobiles were predominantly black, our walls were tan, garments were largely black or white, factory walls were whitewashed or made a dismal gray like the machines. In ancient times dyes and pigments were so precious they were used as currency, kings' ransoms, and royal gifts. Only a rich man could afford colored garments and the more they reeked of strong dyes, the greater was the sign of his wealth and importance.

In early Colonial days in America, housewives were noted for their particular formulas for certain dyes. When other housewives wanted their yarns dyed they would take some to "Mrs. Jones" to have them dyed brown, to "Mrs. Smith" for some to be dyed red, others to "Mrs. Bailey" to have them dyed yellow. The Colonial storekeeper had only a few bolts of fabric in only a small variety of colors. Today it is sometimes difficult to choose because of the many, many colors in all fabrics. As the knowledge and availability of color increases, so does our demand for an even greater variety of forms and colors in our fabrics, our paints, and our furnishings.

135

One may study color from any one of four scientific approaches.

1. The *physiologist* studies color from the way it is received by the eye. Factory employers have performed fatigue experiments to determine how they could get their employees to produce more work with greater ease by means of color conditioning their surroundings. Color safety codes in some cases cut the accident ratio as much as 45 percent. Colored work areas are planned to reduce eye strain and fatigue, and rest areas are planned in colors for relaxation.

2. The psychologist studies how a person is affected emotionally by the colors he sees and how colors are affected by one another. The "Op" artist has capitalized on the psychological effects of color vibrations caused by closely related values of bright intensities.

The United States Navy has found that submarine crews have better health, morale, and efficiency in spite of their restricted space and long days under the surface when there is beautiful planning of the colors for the submarine interior.

We have become so familiar with judging the quality of food by its color that many sensitive individuals would not enjoy a dinner of purple steak, green butter, blue potatoes, red bread, and chartruese milk. One experiment has dealt with changing the basic color of foods. After eating bright green mashed potatoes, many people were unable to recognize this strange food, even though the taste had not been changed. Psychiatrists tell us that many of our divorces are the result of unsatisfactory color in surroundings. One husband may become irritable and morose if the walls are yellow and brown. A wife may be affected in a similar way by forms of red and blue. Most individuals have color likes and dislikes and are affected emotionally by those hues in their surroundings. Colors that appeal to children may seem garish to adults. Colors that appeal to the underprivileged and uneducated may be entirely different from those that the more cultured or wealthy would choose. This may also be true of nationalities of different temperate zones. Much additional study is needed to better understand the psychological effects of color.

3. The *physicist* studies wavelengths and intensities of light. The experiments by physicists illustrate the fact that colored lights, when mixed, do not produce the same results as would be obtained by mixing

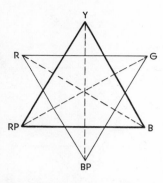

Fig. 6-2 The physicist develops his color theory around a six-hue wheel. In light, the blue-purple is complementary to the yellow, the blue is complementary to the red, and the red-purple is complementary to the green.

pigments of the same hues. The physicist works with light rays, whereas pigments are colored matter of either mineral or vegetable origin. A colored surface absorbs or subtracts from white light and wavelengths of all the colors except its own, and so gives the impression of that particular color. Colored lights may be mixed to form any number of brilliant colors as well as white. In the light theory red, green, and blue-purple are the three primaries instead of the red, blue, and yellow in the pigment theory. The three secondary colors, as they are seen in light, are yellow, red-purple, and blue. These secondaries are produced as follows: yellow light is obtained by mixing red and green lights; red-purple results from mixing red and blue-purple; blue light is secured by mixing green and blue-purple. In Fig. 6-2, the dotted lines connect complementary pairs which will neutralize each other when combined and will produce white light. The lighting engineer for dramatic productions can create color effects with lights by the flick of a switch that would take the painter hours of labor and gallons of paint to achieve. Sometimes whole backgrounds can be entirely changed by the use of different lights. Certain chemicals, such as zinc, phospherine, and radium bromide, can also change the color effects when various lights are reflected on them. They might even change the appearance of a surface from a pattern to a solid color.

4. The *chemist* studies the chemical properties of the natural and artificial coloring materials used for the manufacture of dyes and paints. He knows that pigments mix differently and produce different hues from mixtures of colored lights. He experiments with definite formulas for mixing paints so one may be assured of always being able to match a particular color. He tests problems of fading, washing, cracking, peeling, and spreading consistencies. He seeks new sources of pigments and dyes. The Prang color theory explained in this text is an example of pigment mixtures.

A number of systems for the organization of color have been devised. Two are in common use today: the Prang System and the Munsell System. In this text only the Prang theory will be discussed in detail. For further study and comparison of the two systems it is suggested that the reader use Munsell's *Color Atlas and Color Notation* and *A Practical Description of the Munsell Color System* by T. M. Cleland.

THE PRANG COLOR SYSTEM

We need some way of describing the general characteristics of color. For this reason the three ways in which colors may be said to differ are in their *hue*, *value*, and *intensity*. These terms are referred to synonomously as *properties*, *qualities*, or *dimensions* of color.

1. *Hue*—the name of the color, such as red or blue-green.
2. *Value*—the lightness or darkness of the color.
3. *Intensity*—the brightness or dullness of the color.

All these dimensions may be used to describe every form of color, just as height, width, and depth may be used to describe an object.

HUE

Hues may be classified in a number of different ways.

Warm and Cool Hues. Those hues that have varying amounts of the red that we associate with fire are identified as warm, whereas those that have differing amounts of blue in them give more the effect of coolness. Colors which are on the borderline are yellow and violet. Yellow appears more warm because of its association with sunshine, and more cool because of its lightness in value. Violet is a mixture of both red and blue. Warm hues are more advancing and make objects appear larger, whereas cool ones are more receding and decrease apparent size. This could be used to advantage in an interior. If a room is small, cool hues might make it seem larger, whereas large areas of warm hues could possibly make it seem still smaller.

Arrangement on the Color Wheel. Hues may be classified as primary, secondary, or binary, and intermediate for purposes of organization on a color wheel. In Fig. 6-3 note that the heavy line connecting the primary hues of red, blue, and yellow form an equilateral triangle. These hues are the ones which are most important. No other hues can be mixed to obtain them. They are the basis for all other forms of color.

The finer line connecting the secondary hues of green, orange, and

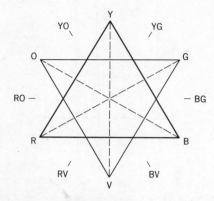

Fig. 6-3 Prang develops his color theory around a twelve-hue circle. The heavy line connects the primary hues; the fine line connects the secondary hues; and the intermediate hues are shown in between each of the primary and secondary hues.

Color Wheel

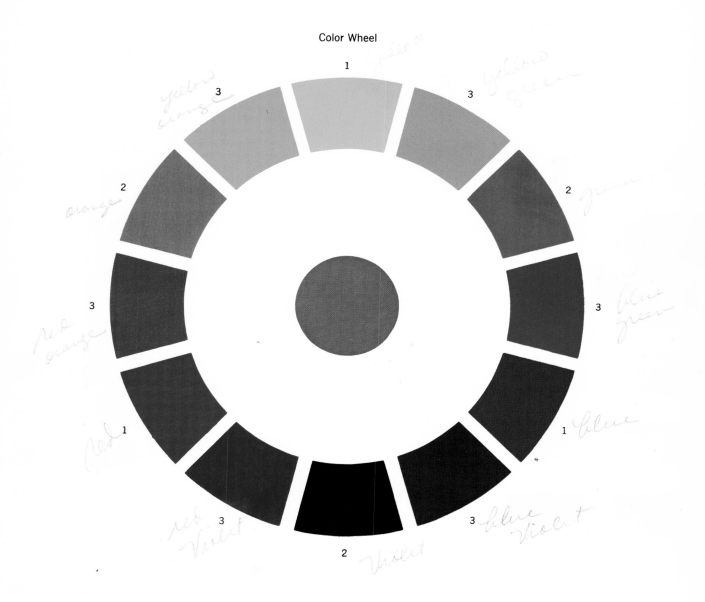

Fig. 6-11   The Prang color wheel is divided into three groups of hues. Those marked (1) are the Primary hues; those marked (2) are the Secondary hues; those marked (3) indicate the Intermediate hues. Reading clockwise around the circle, the colors are: Yellow, yellow-green, green, blue-green, blue, blue-violet, violet, red-violet, red, red-orange, orange, and yellow-orange.

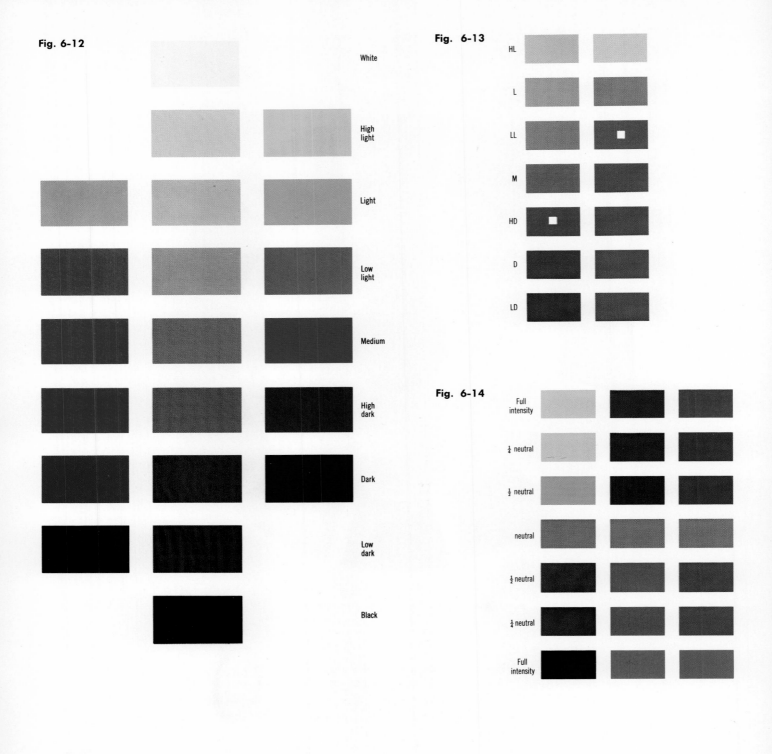

Fig. 6-12

White

High light

Light

Low light

Medium

High dark

Dark

Low dark

Black

Fig. 6-13

HL

L

LL

M

HD

D

LD

Fig. 6-14

Full intensity

¼ neutral

½ neutral

neutral

½ neutral

¼ neutral

Full intensity

(extreme left)
Fig. 6-12 Normal value scale. Standard value scale with the normal equivalents in hues shown in relation to the steps on the value scale.

(upper right)
Fig. 6-13 Value scale of red and orange. Each hue has a normal value (the one with the white square) and may be raised or lowered from the normal value.

(lower right)
Fig. 6-14 Intensity scale. Each hue may be changed in intensity by adding the complement until the neutral gray is reached.

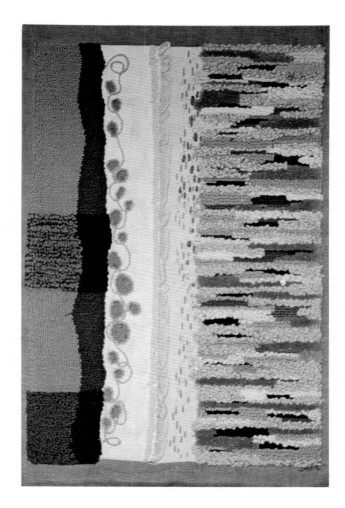

Fig. 6-15 Monochromatic hues of different values of yellow with neutral gray, white, and black. (Designed by Ethel Jane Beitler. Photograph by Billie Wolfe.)

Fig. 6-16 Analogous hues of yello[w],
green, and blue-green in reverse or[der]
of values. (Designed by Ethel J[ane]
Beitler. Photograph by Billie Wol[fe.])

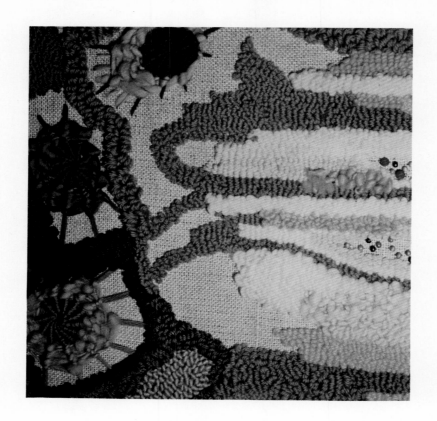

Fig. 6-17 Detail of stitchery wallpie[ce]
shown above. (Designed by Ethel Ja[ne]
Beitler. Photograph by Billie Wolfe.)

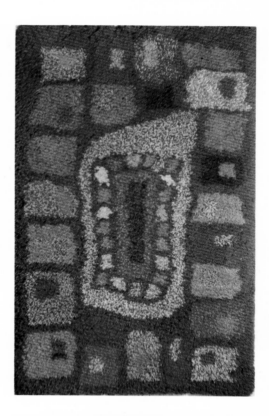

Fig. 6-18   Analogous hues of yellow, green, and blue-green in reverse of the natural order of values, with neutral gray and black. (Made by Dr. Foster Marlow, Head, Department of Art, Southwestern Texas State College.)

Fig. 6-19   ''Firelight on the Hearthstones,'' a knotted area rug, radiates the warm analogous hues in reverse order of values. (Made by Mrs. Mattie Smithee, Lubbock, Texas. Photograph by Billie Wolfe.)

Fig. 6-20   Complementary hues of blue and orange made more pleasing with different values of each.

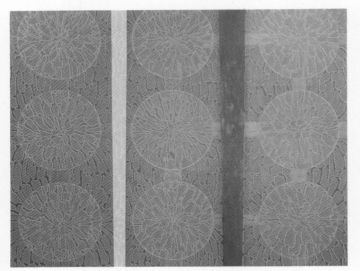

Fig. 6-21 The double-complement allows one to combine more hues in varying amounts. (Made by Juanita Pollard.)

Fig. 6-22 A triad color collage for a family room. (Dark yellow carpet from Jack Harvey Carpet Company, Lubbock, Texas. Pale yellow walls and drapery, solid blue and red upholstery for chairs and floor cushions, print sofa fabric in red and blue from Boris Kroll Fabrics, Inc., New York, New York.)

Fig. 6-23 A triad color combination for a painting. (Photograph courtesy of Mr. Hugh Gibbons.)

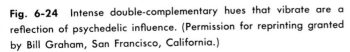

Fig. 6-24 Intense double-complementary hues that vibrate are a reflection of psychedelic influence. (Permission for reprinting granted by Bill Graham, San Francisco, California.)

Fig. 6-25 Reverse order of values of complementary hues is used for dramatic effect. (Permission for reprinting granted by Bill Graham, San Francisco, California.)

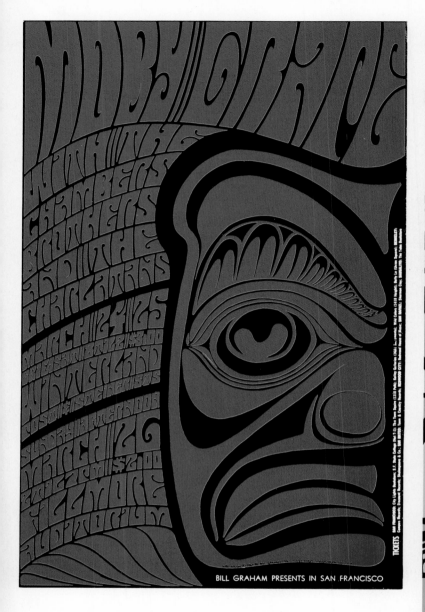

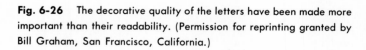

BILL GRAHAM PRESENTS IN SAN FRANCISCO

Fig. 6-26 The decorative quality of the letters have been made more important than their readability. (Permission for reprinting granted by Bill Graham, San Francisco, California.)

Fig. 6-27 The lettering and illustration have been planned as one related unit in the highly decorative psychedelic design. (Permission for reprinting granted by Bill Graham, San Francisco, California.)

violet also form an equilateral triangle. The green is placed half-way between the yellow and blue because equal amounts of yellow and blue are mixed to make green. Equal amounts of blue and red are mixed to make violet, and also equal amounts of red and yellow make orange. Actually the equal mixing of two primary colors to make a secondary color works in theory. You will find many of the paints you purchase will not mix to make a true and accurate color.

Each intermediate hue has a compound name composed of the primary and secondary hues which are used to mix it. For instance, yellow-green is a mixture of the primary yellow and the secondary green. Blue-green is a mixture of the primary blue and the secondary green. You may produce each intermediate hue by the mixture of a primary and secondary hue and it is placed half-way between these hues. If you were to mix the primary and secondary hues (for instance, yellow and green) there would be any number of different proportions of the two that you might use, but the resulting hue would still be classified in this case as yellow-green. It might be identified as a yellow yellow-green, a yellow-green, or a green yellow-green. See Figs. 6-3 and 6-11. Munsell has a notation system which enables one to determine the approximate amount of yellow and green that is present in the yellow-green, but Prang has no set formula or system for identification of each variation of the intermediate hues.

Normal, Standard, and Popular Hues. A hue which is a pure pigment is known as a *normal* hue. For practical purposes Prang has indicated only twelve normal hues on his color circle, but it would be possible with the many variations of intermediate hues to recognize approximately one hundred different normal hues. A hue is changed into another hue by adding a neighboring primary or secondary hue to it. For example, yellow plus green equals yellow-green, or yellow plus blue equals green. Or a transparent film of a neighboring hue may be placed over the original hue to change the appearance of both hues.

The six normal hues which are most frequently used are classified as standard hues and are the ones usually found in a child's box of paints. They are red, yellow, blue, green, orange, and violet. In the pigment theory of color, black, gray, and white are not classified as hues but as neutrals. The *neutrals* will be discussed under the heading of "value." Many familiar names of colors do not appear on the color wheel. Pink, lavender, tan, brown, beige are names which are given to various values and intensities of colors. Most of these *popular* names of colors are coined by manufacturers for the purpose of advertising their merchandise each season. The various forms of colors take on new fashionable connotations and cause others to become "dated" and unpopular. For instance, one season the fashionable color might be "Evergreen," a dark value and moderately grayed form of green. Another season a similar type of green, except perhaps a bit darker in value, might be referred to as "Forest Green."

If one has a thorough understanding of the dimension of hue, he should be able to:

1. Describe the color as far as its proper name and location on the color wheel.
2. Recognize its advancing and receding properties.
3. Recognize its qualities of warmth and coolness.

VALUE

The second dimension of color is value, or the variation in darkness and lightness. If one were to add varying amounts of black to white one could recognize many different degrees of darkness and lightness. For practical purposes, however, we usually use only seven values of gray in between the white and the black. These are arranged in regular manner in a chart referred to as a *Value Scale*. (See chart in Fig. 6-4 and 6-5.) This scale shows the neutral in the center with the equivalent normal hues in relation to each value of gray. No color can be as light as white or as dark as black. If one were to draw a line between each pair of colors, as in Fig. 6-3, one could see how the hues, as they are arranged on the color wheel, fall automatically in the same arrangement as they are placed on the value scale. You will also note, therefore, that the normal hues show a natural variation in darkness and lightness. For instance, yellow is the lightest and is placed as the equivalent of the high-light in value. Yellow-green and yellow-orange are darker and are placed as the equivalent of light. Green and orange are still darker and are placed as the equivalent of low-light,

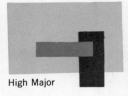

High Major

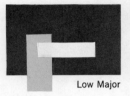

Low Major

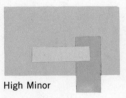

High Minor

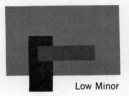

Low Minor

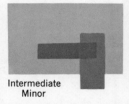

Intermediate
Minor

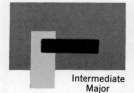

Intermediate
Major

Fig. 6-4

Fig. 6-5 High-minor value key. (Student design.)

and so on to violet which is the equivalent of low-dark. See Fig. 6-12.

You will also discover that the value of each normal hue may be changed by the addition of white or water (in water-base paints) to raise the value, or black to lower the value. Thus, a *tint* is any value above normal and a *shade* is any value below normal for that particular hue. For example, adding a small amount of white to violet would produce a tint of violet even though this tint would fall as the equivalent of dark or high-dark on the value scale. It is possible to raise the value of every hue to a value just under white, and lower it to a value just above black. For practical purposes, a value of yellow above high-light and a value of violet below low-dark would not be included on the standard chart, but it would be possible to recognize those values with the eye. See Fig. 6-13.

Value Keys. In choosing the various values to be used together in a particular composition a series of value keys have been developed to aid the student in making reference to or describing a particular arrangement of values. These "keys" utilize the terms "major" and "minor." "Major" signifies strong contrast of values, while "minor" signifies little contrast or the same values. We mentioned earlier in this chapter that values above medium were referred to as "high values" and those below medium as "low values." Therefore, by combining these terms with the words "major" and "minor" we can arrive at the following "value keys." (See Fig. 6-4.)

1. *High major key.* Strong contrast of dark and light values with at least five steps difference in values with high values (above medium) occupying a larger area than the low values. (They may be any hue or neutrals.)

2. *Low major key.* Strong contrast of dark and light values with at least five steps difference in values with low values (below medium) occupying a larger area than the high values. (They may be any hue or neutrals.)

3. *High minor key.* Same or similar values with no more than three steps apart on the value scale, and all above medium in value. (They may be any hue or neutrals.)

4. *Low minor key.* Same or similar values with no more than three steps apart on the value scale, and all below medium in value. (They may be any hue or neutrals.)

5. *Intermediate minor key.* Same or similar values with no more than

Fig. 6-6 Color lends itself in each of the dimensions to expressions of rhythm. This student experiment shows gradations of size, gradation of hues of red-orange, orange, yellow-orange, and black, gradation of values, and also gradation of intensities. Low-major value key. (Student design.)

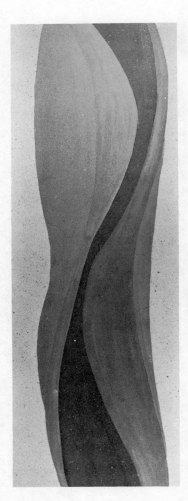

Fig. 6-7 A student experiment for a rug design shows graceful *sweeping rhythms* in a pleasing *gradation of hues* of yellow-orange, orange, and red-orange. Intermediate-major value key.

three steps apart on the value scale, and all in the middle part of the value scale. (They may be any hue or neutrals.)

6. *Intermediate major key.* Strong contrast of dark and light values with at least five steps difference in values occupying the largest area of medium value (They may be any hue or neutrals.)

For applications of a few of the value keys see Figs. 6-5, 6-6, and 6-7.

Order of Values. The standard value scale with its equivalent normal hues becomes a very valuable chart to keep in mind when combining different values of colors. There are those combinations in which the colors seem to have a natural affinity for each other, and there are those which have a quality of strangeness about them. The latter does not mean they do not harmonize but rather that they represent a more unusual and intriguing selection of hues. When we refer to the "*natural order of values*" we mean that we have selected the values of the hues used together in the *same order of values* that they are found on the value scale. This does not mean that they must be in these same values. For instance, the normal green is placed at low-light, whereas the normal

142

blue-green falls at medium. If we use the two hues together in the natural order of values, all that is meant is that the green will be lighter than the blue-green. We would still have a wide range of possible values of both hues which could be used together and still select a value of green that would be lighter than the blue-green. We might use a high-light green with a low-light blue-green—or a high-light green with a low-dark blue-green. As long as the green is lighter than the blue-green, it would be a natural order of values.

If we reverse those values and use the blue-green lighter than the green, then it becomes "reverse order of values" and we find they do not have that natural affinity for each other and need to be planned more carefully.

To illustrate, we might use an example far removed from the subject of color. Not all persons get along well together. They may clash because of personality differences, their personal interests may be so different that they have no common interests, they may have racial prejudices. Whatever the reasons for their disagreements, they may still live together in the same community and get along with each other in peace providing they observe certain courtesies. They may see each other only occasionally and thus be able to keep from getting on each other's nerves. Or their interests may be so different that they appeal to each other even more because of their differences. With our color combinations of reverse order of values, one way to make them harmonize—or get along well together—is

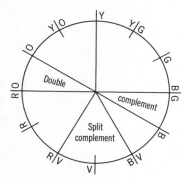

Fig. 6-8 Neighboring hues are *analogous.*

Fig. 6-9 Hues directly across from each other are complementary. (O and B, BG and RO). The four together form a double-complement. The *split*-complement has *one hue* with *two forms of its complement,* as (Y with RV and BV).

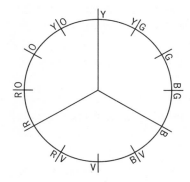

Fig. 6-10 The triad is composed of three hues equally distant, as (R, Y, and B).

to use only a small amount of the reverse value with a large amount of the other colors, or have the values and intensities decidedly different from each other. When they are so similar, they may be just enough different to compete for attention and spoil the whole effect of harmony. See Fig. 6-16, 17 & 18. The blue-green is light in value and relatively bright in intensity, while the green is dark in value and dull in intensity. Reverse order of value may be more effective when more hues are used in one design.

Reverse order of values can also be compared to dissonance in music. Frequently a melody in minor key is much more haunting and beautiful than one in a more ordinary major key. The technique of singing or playing a musical instrument in a minor key takes more skill to know just how much off-key to pitch a note and have it sound "right." Contemporary composers of music by using dissonance to produce a "just right" off-key combination of tones give a dramatic, intriguing, or haunting quality. This is a drastic change from compositions of the past such as a Strauss waltz. These compositions were developed around major key sounds. In the twentieth century, composers such as Arnold Schoenberg and Ernst Krenek, favor the use of the 12-tone scale over the major and minor modes in which various combinations of intervals produce total dissonance. It is further seen that the half-step interval of the 12-tone scale is once again divided to produce quarter-tone intervals as in the string compositions of Alois Haba. In music, to a person whose ear is not attuned to the appreciation of dissonance the sounds may appear as discord. In color, a combination of hues in reverse order of values may in turn appear as discord to the person who is not sensitive to the dramatic possibilities of these "off-key" hues.

If one has a thorough understanding of the dimension of value, he should be able to:

1. Name the steps on the standard value scale with the equivalent normal hues in relation to them.

2. Raise or lower the value of any hue.

3. Identify the step on the value scale to which a hue has been changed.

4. Identify the value key which has been used in a composition.

INTENSITY

The third dimension of color is intensity or chroma—the variation in brightness and dullness—its strength or its weakness. Value is the dimension that enables a color to speak in a very dainty, quiet manner, or in a heavy, gentlemanly tone. Intensity is the property that enables it to shout in a shrill, vibrant tone or in a quiet, dignified, or somber manner. The normal hues are the ones which are the brightest that it is possible for a color to be. The grayed forms are the ones which are closer to the neutral. To lower the intensity we can add the complement which is the color directly across from it, the line connecting the two going through the center of the circle, or add a neutral of gray, black, or white. For instance, yellow is the complement of violet; red is the complement of green; yellow-green is the complement of red-violet. When the complement is added to a color, the normal reaction is not only to gray the color but also to make it darker in value. (see Fig. 6-14). If one wishes to add the complement and keep the value constant, neutral white needs to be added also. As the complement is added to the color, there is a midpoint between the two where the resulting color is a neutral. For example, if one adds green to red to make a dull red, by adding increasing amounts of green we reach the midpoint where both the red and green are destroyed by each other and every other addition of green thereafter would result in a grayed green rather than a grayed red.

The reason the word "complement" is used is because it is derived from the word "complete." For instance, in the complementary combination of red and green we note that red is one of the primary hues. Green is a mixture of blue and yellow, the two other primaries. Thus, in the combination, we have used all three of the primary hues. This is true of each pair of hues which are directly across from each other on the color wheel and which we designate as complementary hues. When we lower or raise the value of a color we can indicate the step on the value scale to which it would be equivalent. Then we would have a relatively good idea of the degree of darkness and lightness of the resulting color. When we lower the intensity of a color, however, we do not have as satisfactory a way of identifying the particular degree of intensity to which the color has been lowered. Through experimentation and practice, we are able to recognize when a color has been grayed only slightly, or made very dull, or various degrees in between. The Prang notation system expresses forms of colors in the following manner:

1. Hue is indicated by the initials of the color as R for red, or YG for yellow-green.

2. Value is indicated by the name of the initials of the step to which it corresponds on the value scale as high-light or HL. Thus red at high-light would be indicated as R HL.

3. Intensity is expressed as a fraction or a percentage of its degree of neutralization, as $\frac{1}{4}$N or 25%N. Thus a slightly grayed, high-light red would be designated as R HL $\frac{1}{4}$N, or R HL 25%N. One that is very dull and low-dark might be indicated as R LD $\frac{7}{8}$N, or R LD 87%N (see Fig. 6-6).

It would be wise for one making a study of color to make a series of gradations of hue, value, and intensity of several hues, and arrange them in a comparative chart. By actually mixing pigments, one can see the reaction which takes place and be able to recognize similar forms of colors already mixed, as in printed fabrics.

Effects of brightness or dullness may be varied by means of different textures. A shiny texture reflects light, whereas a dull one absorbs it. Therefore if two fabrics, a shiny polished cotton and a rough weave cotton boucle, were both put into the same dye bath, the polished cotton would appear brighter in intensity. The rough weave would soften the intensity of the color and make it seem duller. This is one of the reasons why a large person should be careful in choosing a shiny textured fabric, especially in bright intensities. It would make her seem even larger in scale and call attention to her size.

Complementary hues, placed in juxtaposition, especially bright in intensity, tend to emphasize each other. Observe packages of meat in the supermarket—the sprig of green parsley or rings of green pepper make the meat appear redder and more delicious.

Law of Areas. To make various color harmonies one should be aware of what is sometimes referred to as the "Law of Areas"—the "Law of Backgrounds." This "law" states that the largest area should be quiet in effect with small accents of bright intensities. Gradually over many centuries we have become more accustomed to more noise in our surroundings—motors, horns, bells, machines all clammering at once. The more noise we have, the more resistance we build up for it, so that we do not notice the noise. The colors we use in our homes, our advertising, our wearing apparel are gradually showing brighter intensities. What is grayed to us might have seemed bright to former generations. However, in spite of all this, we still follow, in our own relative way, the Law of Areas, especially for color combinations for large areas such as rooms in homes. One of the most common violations of the Law of Areas is our use of equal amounts of bright red and bright green for Christmas decorations. Some people defend this combination because it is traditionally Christmas. Actually the green of Christmas comes from the evergreen which is both a dark and dulled green. The red comes from the tiny red berries. The larger areas are then the dark dull green, accented with the small areas of bright red. Nature seems always to follow the Law of Areas. The Law of Areas does not deal with the property of value, for one may use a large area of light value with a small area of dark value, or vice versa.

If one has a thorough understanding of the dimension of intensity, he should be able to:

1. Recognize the forcefulness of bright intensities and use them wisely. Follow the Law of Areas.

2. Change the intensities of colors by the addition of the complement or neutral.

3. Change the intensity of colors and still keep the value constant.

4. Make a color appear to be more intense by placing it beside some of its complementary hue.

5. Make a color appear to be more intense by placing beside it more of the same hue in a duller intensity.

6. Make a color appear to be less intense by placing beside it a very dull related hue about the same value.

We may summarize the discussions of hue, value, and intensity in the form of charts such as the ones shown in Figs. 6-13 and 6-14. Any hue may be changed in value and intensity. A hue that has progressive amounts of white added to it is still the same hue, but it becomes a lighter and lighter *tint*. As black is added, it is still the same hue, but it becomes a darker and darker *shade*. Through the center part of the diagram we note that the *intensity* is being changed by the addition of the complement. As more and more of the complement is added we approach the midpoint of gray. This works in theory with some brands of paints, but with others it is practically impossible to get a neutral gray, probably due to the mixtures of the pigment formulas.

It is very difficult to carry the exact value and intensity of a color in our minds when we go to a shop to buy paint, wallpaper, fabrics, etc. when we wish to match something we already have. If we are asked to match a particular hue without carrying a sample with us, we will usually select a darker value of the same hue. When judging a definite value, a lighter value will probably be chosen. And when we are striving to match a certain intensity, a brighter one will very likely be selected.

MECHANICAL COLOR SCHEMES

Some students of color may wish to have some more or less specific starting points for planning their color combinations. Color preferences, of course, may be influenced by many factors. One factor might be the amount of light. Where sunlight is abundant, the colors people choose are inclined to be strong, rich, and more brilliant. Where there is little sunlight, softer colors are wanted with duller and cooler ones preferred.

Merchants who deal with colored items must consider very carefully whether they are dealing with clients who will want "high fashion" colors or whether their clients belong to the larger mass of the population who are on a fairly lean budget, have simple tastes, and feel that they must hold to a single color range rather than the strange, off-shades of the more sophisticated individuals. The mass public knows what it likes and prefers to stick to it. Their style trends are slow to change. It is better for the manufacturer to suggest many styles in a few color ranges than a few styles in many color ranges. In high-fashion circles, the desire is to avoid the commonplace. They are inclined to try to coordinate more unusual kinds of colors with related products. For instance, an expensive brand of perfume might be boxed in a brilliant fuschia, or a silk throw pillow might be a rich olive green. The style trends change rapidly and

148

there must be constant prognostication of trends in colors to coordinate the new colors with the new products being manufactured.

We stress the fact that every color in all its values and intensities is beautiful. It is just a problem of deciding which value or intensity should be used for the purpose and how large an area to use. That, however, is a big order. We may begin by studying other combinations which have been used in pictures, fabrics, homes, store windows, magazines. Many times, however, a color scheme may look beautiful in one place but not be so fine when repeated for the purpose for which we need the colors. One way to begin to study color might be to get some colored papers or paint chips or fabrics and try various arrangements. Another way to begin might be to divide the color wheel into two main groups: related hues and contrasting hues. We may then plan some subheadings under each of these so our outline would be as follows:

A. Related hues
  1. Monochromatic
  2. Analogous
  3. Accented neutral
B. Contrasting hues
  1. Complementary
     (a) Simple complement
     (b) Split-complement
     (c) Double-complement
  2. Triad

Related hues have a color in common. They are classified as the same or similar in hue. "Mono-" means "one" and "chroma" means "color-intensity." Thus a monochromatic color scheme has come to mean different values or intensities of one color. There are a number of suggestions that might aid one in making a more interesting color harmony with only one color, but these suggestions will all be grouped together at the end of this chapter as many of them could be applied to all types of color schemes. See Fig. 6-15 for an example of different values of one hue of yellow plus the neutrals of gray, black, and white.

Analogous hues are those that lie next to each other or near each other on the color wheel. They have a color in common. For instance, yellow-green, green, and blue-green all have green in common. We could also say they have yellow in common. If we went further around the color wheel we might add yellow, yellow-orange, and orange and still be able to say they all have yellow in common. However, it is usually wise, for analogous compositions, to limit the selection of hues to those which lie either between two primaries or two secondaries. See Figs. 6-16, 6-17, and 6-18. Yellow, yellow-green, and blue-green have been used in interesting examples of reverse order of values. In Fig. 6-19 the warm hues of red, red-orange, and red-violet produce a vibrant combination for an area rug.

We have already discussed earlier in this chapter the fact that complementary hues are those which lie across from each other on the color wheel, the line connecting them going through the center of the circle. Sometimes, for the sake of variety, we wish to add another hue, or more unusual forms. For instance, instead of using red and green we may wish to use the yellow-green and blue-green on either side of the green with the red. This is referred to as a *split-complement*. When we have need of a still greater variety of hues, two sets of complements, like yellow-green and red-violet, blue-green and red-orange, could be used, and thus classified as a *double-complement*.

In Fig. 6-9 a simple diagram indicates locations on the color wheel of simple, double, and split complementary color combinations. In Fig. 6-20 a simple complement of blue and orange have been given added interest because of the two values of each which have been used together. In Fig. 6-21 a double complement gives a greater variety of hues of red, red-violet, green and yellow-orange to use together for a canvas.

Triad hues are those which are equally distant on the color wheel. Each set forms an equilateral triangle, as in red, yellow, blue—green, orange, violet—yellow-green, red-orange, blue-violet—yellow-orange, red-violet, blue-green. In Fig. 6-23 a triad of yellow, red, and blue have been assembled for a contemporary canvas, while in Fig. 6-22 a collage of the same hues has been arranged for suggestions for colors for a family room: dark, grayed yellow carpet, pale yellow walls and drapery, printed fabric for sofa in red and blue, with red and blue repeated in solid colors for occasional chairs and floor cushions.

The accented neutral scheme could be classified under related hues because only one hue need be used as the accent for large areas of neutral gray, black, or white. Neutrals are not classified literally as hues. The accented neutral might also be classified under the contrasting color schemes because of the contrast between the hue and the neutral.

SUGGESTIONS FOR PLANNING PLEASING COLOR HARMONIES

Just because we select hues from particular locations on the color wheel is no assurance that the result will be a beautiful color harmony. Two colors have been described as being in harmony when each looks better or happier when viewed together. Each color in a harmony has the effect of making the other color more attractive. Many times one color may seem exciting and enjoyable by itself. However, by placing the color next to another color, it suddenly becomes interesting. You should remember that a good colorist can take any guide or rule and develop a seemingly successful color harmony. The following are suggestions for helping you in planning more pleasing color harmonies:

1. Any combination of colors can be made either pleasant or unpleasant, owing to the choice of values and intensities. For instance, blue and orange may be unattractive and uninteresting if used as they are found on the color wheel. On the other hand, they may be very interesting if both of the colors are dulled somewhat (one dulled more than the other) and also if there is some difference in darkness and lightness.

2. Colors usually appear best when they are kept in the same value relationship as that in which they are found on the value scale (natural order of values). If reverse order of values is used, remember to use contrast of value or intensity, or both, and vary the sizes of the areas. This will more likely result in pleasing dissonance.

3. A color harmony should have a dominant color, light or dark effect, warm or cool effect, and/or a combination of these.

4. Dulled warm colors of light values generally are a better background

for a room than are cool colors, because warm colors seem to draw together and unify colors placed against them. Cool colors as backgrounds seem to separate colors placed against them.

5. Background colors should follow the principle of the Law of Areas. Intense colors should be used as small accents. The smaller the area, the brighter their color may be.

6. All light values which are also all rather bright are apt to give a very weak, immature, and uninteresting effect. When all dark values are used together the result may appear depressing and old.

7. A very bright color and a very dull color, both the same value, are seldom very attractive when used together. (The bright color will often look unrefined and garish, whereas the dull color will seem muddy and drab.)

8. A group of colors in which all colors are of pure intensity (even though some variety in darkness and lightness may be present) often looks unrefined and primitive.

9. The more contrast there is in value, the more "exciting" and "dramatic" the combinations. When too much contrast is used, however, the result is apt to be confusing and lacking in unity.

10. When it is impossible to match exactly the hue, value, and intensity, a slight variation of hue, value, and intensity is preferable.

CREATIVE EXPERIMENTS

1. To develop an awareness of color in everyday surroundings:

   a. Check through the "color glossary" at the end of this book and find in magazines as many examples as you can of color combinations illustrating the terms in the glossary.
   b. Find examples of color combinations which illustrate the following words: melancholy, gaiety, anger, quietness.

2. To experiment with color in a creative manner:

   a. Make a chart to show examples of change of hue, value, and intensity.
   b. Use colored papers and plan three small abstract designs.

    (1) Repeat the design four times on one plate illustrating:
       (a) Related hues
       (b) Contrasting hues
       (c) Warm hues
       (d) Cool hues
    (2) Repeat the second design four times on one plate illustrating:
       (a) High major key
       (b) High minor key
       (c) Low major key
       (d) Low minor key
    (3) Repeat the third design four times on one plate illustrating:
       (a) Bright intensities
       (b) Dull intensities
       (c) Slightly grayed intensities
       (d) Law of Areas

c. Plan a composition expressing rhythm and paint it, using different values of one color.

d. Repeat the design in (c) using different values of related hues.

e. Plan a simple geometric design and trace it four times. Paint each to illustrate:
    (1) Related hues and related values
    (2) Related hues and contrasting values
    (3) Complementary hues and reverse order of values
    (4) Triad hues and law of areas

f. Plan a simple abstract design to suggest modern industry. Select colors which will carry out the theme of the design.

g. Listen to a record and let the melody suggest a design. Complete the design with colors which carry out the theme of the music.

7

FEELING IS SEEING

Fig. 7-1 Sun shining on the weathered timbers supporting the roof of the old adobe building emphasizes the cracks in the logs and the roughness of texture of the adobe. (Photograph by Bill Crump.)

Sales personnel are urged by their employers to "get the merchandise into the customer's hands—let her *feel* it." Feeling is seeing. A desire for the article grows stronger as she handles it, views it from all angles, imagines it in her own home. Students in some foreign lands are frequently blindfolded and required to feel objects of art or feel them under a protective covering of cloth so there will not be the temptation to look at the object at the same time they feel it. Thus the tactile sense is developed to a high degree, and as a result the visual sense is also strengthened. We refer to depth, width, and height of a form; the hue, value, and intensity of a color. Differences in texture can be referred to as smooth, rough, slippery, soft, silky, fuzzy, sharp, and many other adjectives as we become more aware of the variations of the surfaces which we touch.

Youngsters are constantly cautioned by their elders, "Don't touch;" whereas if they were taught *how* to touch, they would develop an appreciation early in life for all phases of beauty.

See Figs. 7-1 through 7-11 for examples of a variety of textures found in nature. Fig. 7-12 shows an interesting man-made textural effect obtained by lifting oil from the surface of water onto a piece of paper.

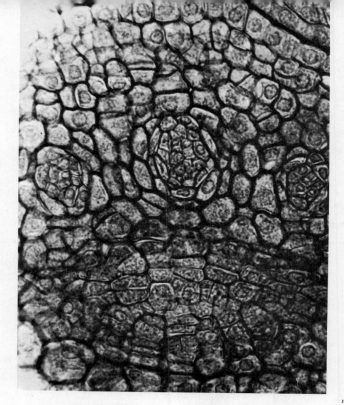

Fig. 7-2 Photomicrograph of the transverse section of a young leaf and axillary bud of yucca. (Photograph courtesy of Dr. Earl D. Camp, Chairman, Dept. of Biology, Texas Tech University.)

Fig. 7-3 Photomicrograph of the transverse section of a leaf blade. (Photograph courtesy of Dr. Earl D. Camp, Chairman, Dept. of Biology, Texas Tech University.)

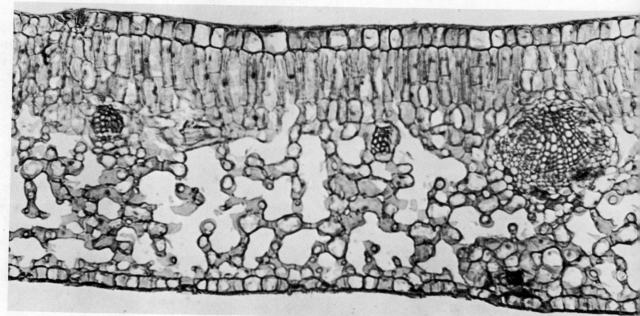

TEXTURE VERSUS PATTERN VERSUS FORM

It may be interesting to try to distinguish just where texture, pattern, and form begin and end. For instance, a brick has a certain roughness about it when we run a hand over its surface. A brick wall which has had the bricks arranged in a particular manner might take on a pattern of long and short areas, with the mortar between giving a variation in the height of the larger surface. Occasionally the bricklayer might place the form of a whole brick in a projecting manner for additional individuality. In doing so, the regularity of pattern is changed, but so is the texture of the entire wall area.

Note the photographs of Yucatan stone shown in Figs. 7–13*a*, *b*, and *c*. In (*a*) there is no particular variation in height that is evident except that which is due to the coarseness of the ingredients in the stone. In (*b*), however, the stone has been shaped in a mold which shows a slight variation in the heights of the various parts of the stone, arranged in a regular pattern. In (*c*) a decided variation in the heights of the areas of the stone create a geometric pattern of high and low rectangles and squares.

Fig. 7-4 Textures of some woods become very rough and linear in character as the branch is exposed to the ravages of wind and rain.

Fig. 7-5 Textures of other woods are smooth and polished, resembling the leathery skin of an elderly individual who has spent many years in the out-of-doors.

(top left)

Fig. 7-6 Wood shavings and sawdust have a brittle or crumbly texture.

(bottom left)

Fig. 7-7 The texture of the handmade blocks is rough from the mixture of mud and straw, dried in the sun and weathered with years. (Photograph by Bill Crump.)

Fig. 7-8 Other bark textures are less rough and ridged and show small areas of smoothness which contrast with the roughness.

When repeated over a large area, such as the exterior wall of a building, the pattern would give a decidedly rough textured and very decorative effect to the building.

An airplane view of a plowed field may give an impression of ridges and undulating irregularities in the surface contour of the field. As we fly closer to the field we can discern the pattern made by the furrows on the flat areas and on the slopes. As we walk in the field we are conscious of the degree of the angle of slope in the furrows, the shapes of the leaves of the plants growing in the field. Thus we see that the study of texture is a relative one and is closely linked with the study of all the other elements: line, shape, form, color, and space.

In general, we say that texture is the *surface quality of an object*. It deals most directly with the sense of touch, although we see much more on the surface because we are aware of how it *feels*. A cabinetmaker runs his hand over a piece of furniture to determine its quality by the finish that has been given to it. He evaluates the proportions of the shape and

Fig. 7-9 Dried coral looks soft, spongy, and lacy, but actually is hard and rough to the touch.

the method of construction, but the first and final test is in the feel of the surface. It must feel smooth, hard, and rich. The dressmaker handles the fabric between her fingers, crushes it, lets it fall from her hand in a draping postion, gets the feel of the "hand" of the fabric. The particular arrangement of yarns in the weave and the blending of colors are important in the evaluation, but the texture itself can be judged manly by the feel.

Imagine, if you can, the delicate softness and fluffiness and almost the feeling of "nothingness" of a handful of dacron filler, then the bulky, yet soft handful of cotton, and then run your hand over a piece of spongy foam rubber. Handle a piece of thin crisp tracing paper, a heavier piece of typing piper of good quality, and a piece of cheap mimeograph paper, and then a piece of lightweight cardboard with a pebbly surface like mat board. We could go on like this, listing hundreds of textures, each with a different surface feel and appearance. These few will suffice to start

160

Fig. 7-10 A combination of textures represented by the riblike veins of the canna leaf enhanced by the crystal-like drops of dew. The shadow pattern in the background also gives a softened texture of highlights and shadows.

Fig. 7-11 The soft furry ears are contrasted with the sharpness of the texture of the grass. ("Princess," owner, Letta Lockhart.)

one thinking of the importance of this element in planning a design. See Figs. 7-14 through 7-18 for a variety of man-made textures.

Looking back over this discussion, we note there are various effects which one may perceive through the element of texture.

1. We appreciate textures from the tactile sense. Their resistance to

162

Fig. 7-12 Immersing a sheet of paper into water on which oil paint has been floated gives a marbleized texture on the paper. Although the results may be quite uncertain, the colors and textures can be very exciting.

pressure may be little or great, causing them to seem soft as down or hard as rocks. When we grasp them between our fingers or run our hands over their surfaces, they appear smooth or rough in varying degrees.

2. We appreciate textures from the visual sense. We see their highlights and shadows caused by their roughness or coarseness. We see their transparancy and their opaqueness. The surface patterns change as we view them in different lights.

3. Textures may also be appreciated by the way they are interpreted

A

B

C

D

Fig. 7-13 *A, B,* and *C.* A variety of textures obtained in Yucatan Stone. (Photographs courtesy of Murals, Inc.) *D,* carved firebrick shows similar roughness of texture of the Yucatan Stone.

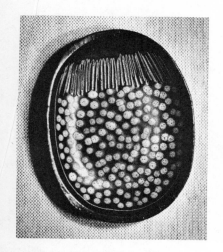

Fig. 7-14 Experimentation with techniques of applying glazes creates unusual textures. (Designers, Jane and Gordon Martz. Courtesy of Marshall Studios, Inc.)

Fig. 7-15 Cast iron may be left rough or relatively smooth for contrast of textures. (Photograph courtesy of Design Today, Inc.)

by the mind of the viewer. They may seem sheer and light and consequently appear to give a dainty impression. Textures that are coarse and rough may appear heavy and bold.

One person may use certain materials, tools, and processes to construct a design. Another person in viewing the design seeks to find a way of interpreting the idea expressed in the design by means of the organization of the lines, colors, shapes, and textures. Without a growing consciousness and discovery of each of these elements the student will find it very difficult to express his ideas to the fullest. See Figs. 7-19 through 7-26 for a variety of other designs which emphasize textures. In studying textures the student needs to *literally feel* and *emotionally express* textural qualities in his design.

How can you express:

1. The sighing of the wind?
2. The moo of a cow?
3. An explosion?
4. An echo far off in a cave?

INTEGRITY OF MATERIALS

During this past generation we have become acquainted with the term "honest expression in the use of materials." Manufacturers have created a host of new materials in the synthetic field. The first reaction to many of them by the average consumer was a negative one unless the material or the article made from it reminded the consumer of that which he was already familiar. But individuals with a sense of integrity and imagination could see the new materials had great promise and wished to see them used in the best ways possible, not just in imitation of old materials. The early makers of linoleum surfaces for floors frequently imitated the design of the grain of wood and printed it on the linoleum. Celluloid manufacturers created the effect of ivory. Hard plastic surfaces today frequently give the effect of wood grain, but it is no longer painted on the surface in imitation but is photographed from the actual wood surface. Thus the consumer has the design of the grain of the wood, the warmth of the wood color, and also has the advantages of the hard plastic which does not scar, mar, stain, and can be easily cleaned but does not have the tactile quality of wood.

Architects and builders appreciate the value of texture to enhance their designs. The early builders exposed the beams in ceilings because it was the quickest and easiest method of construction. They had the choice of the best materials in the uncut forests and consequently the beams deserved to show. As the building industry expanded and materials became more expensive and more scarce, building methods were developed to utilize less expensive materials, covering them with plaster, paint, or wallpaper. We still do this today, of course, but there is also a return to the early idea of exposing building materials and making them a definite part of the decorative pattern of the building. Charles Eames was one of the pioneers. His own home in California is an excellent example of the use of exposed metal framework for both the interior and exterior of the

Fig. 7-16 Techniques of casting plaster in semiflat designs may give variety of texture in the background with the smoothly rounded bird forms. (Photograph courtesy of Design Today, Inc.)

Fig. 7-17 The texture of the highly glazed tiles lend themselves dramatically to strong contrasts of dark and light. (Designed by Evelyn Ackerman for Era Industries.)

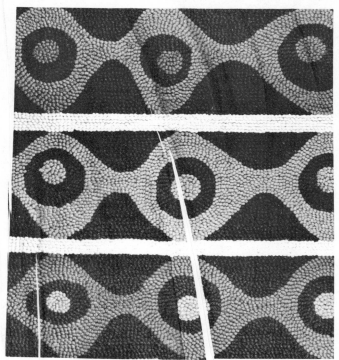

Fig. 7-18 The uncut loops of yarn give a "seedlike" texture to the hooked rug. (Photograph "Seed Pods," Courtesy of Era Industries. Designer, Evelyn Ackerman.)

approx. 2½×6

Fig. 7-19 Smoothly rounded ovals in the grain pattern of wood may suggest to the designer similar patterns to be adapted for rhythmical rug designs.

Fig. 7-20 Seed "painting" of red, yellow, shelled, and dyed millet, poppy seeds and rapeseeds give colorful textural effects for simple, dramatic abstract composition such as the "Bird" by R. Bushlong. (Photographs courtesy of Tom Tru Corp.)

house. Cement blocks are used extensively in many areas for wall construction, letting the rough texture of the blocks form the pattern for both interior and exterior walls. The size and shape of the blocks which are assembled as well as the designs of the molds can be varied in many ways to produce beautiful patterns and textures.

Landscape architects have learned much from the Oriental gardeners concerning the use of natural textures in their compositions. We know that the straight cement walks, the precisely shaped and trimmed shrubs, trees, and lawns may be the more formal and most easily cared for garden. But the rugged beauty of natural rock formations or the casualness of flat discs of wood cut from tree trunks and used for stepping stones or terrace adds more natural beauty of texture to a garden.

VISUAL REPRESENTATION OF TEXTURES

Early painters used their paint in a very smooth, precise manner, but contemporary painters go beyond this. They do not hesitate to use their

169

paint smooth if they wish to create a particular effect, but they also are not afraid to experiment with other ways of using a medium to produce other effects. They may put it on thick with a palette knife, with their fingers, or dab it with a sponge or paper towel, or crush a wire mesh screen on the surface. These textural effects offer wide possibilities for the painter to express himself in whatever way he chooses.

The above paragraph discusses the way a painter may produce actual textures on the surface of his canvas, but the painter may also be concerned with simulating or representing textures in his composition. For instance, if he is painting a portrait, he will wish to show the flesh tones, the texture of the hair, the crisp, filmy, velvety, or wooly texture of the fabric on the model. This representation of various textures is not to be confused with the lack of honesty in the use of materials as discussed earlier in this chapter.

A painter or commercial artist may be concerned with another aspect of representation of texture—that of the effect of light on a surface. The

Fig. 7-21 It may be difficult to distinguish where line, shape, and texture begin and end. They are all interrelated elements which should be enjoyed individually and united as a whole. (Photograph by Bill Crump.)

170

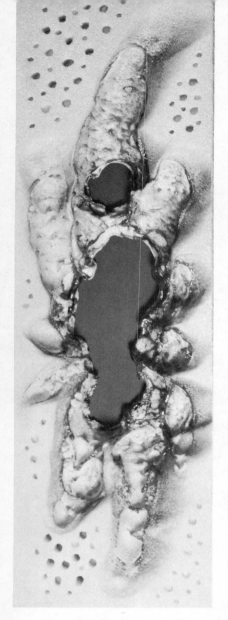

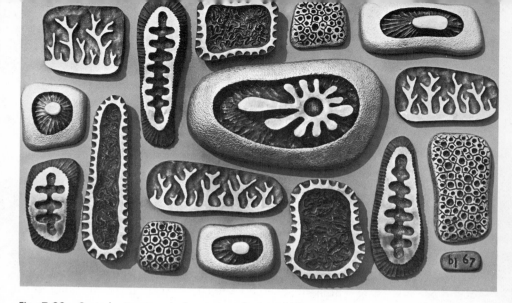

Fig. 7-23 Cast aluminum made from a styrofoam mold becomes a permanent reminder of the styrofoam texture. (Wallpiece designed by Dr. Bill C. Lockhart. Owners, Mr. and Mrs. Jim Steele.)

Fig. 7-22 The welding torch held next to styrofoam causes it to b bble and change to a most exciting textural pattern.

Fig. 7-24 Designs take on an entirely different character when various textures are used. A piece of allover lace was used for the stencilled shapes, creating a very rough, decorative, textural effect. (Student design.)

surface color is broken up by many minute gradations of light and shadow which arrange themselves differently in various textures.

1. Dull or rough textures such as wool or cotton surfaces, wood or stone, absorb light and have an arrangement of closely related values in the light and shadow, representing a high, intermediate, or low minor key.

2. Shiny or smooth textures, such as satin, polished metal, or glass, reflect light and have an arrangement of strong contrast of values in the light and shadow, representing a high major key.

3. Pile fabrics like velvet or corduroy both reflect and absorb light. The arrangement of light and shadow represent a low major key. Every thread of the pile is casting a little shadow on its neighbor so that the reflection on the surface is limited to the topmost tips of the pile.

COMBINATIONS OF TEXTURES

There are no rigid rules or laws concerning the correct combination of textures. One needs to develop a sensitivity to those textures which seem to have a natural affinity for each other. Textures should have something in common or be a pleasant contrast. They may have an air of informality, as an arrangement of zinnias in a copper bowl, placed on a burlap cloth. They may express dainty formality for a reception when an arrangement of iris and tulips in a glass container are placed on an organdy cloth. In each instance the textures seem to repeat the same character. There might, however, be a feeling of interesting contrast such as an interior wall which exposes the natural brick flanked on one side with a window area which is covered with folding panels of opaque plastic in wooden frames like a shojii screen. On the other side of the brick wall might be a solid color drapery of a smooth but not shiny cotton weave. The wood paneling in the built-in cabinets nearby show the fine grain of mahogony rubbed to a rich smoothness. Only the tweed carpeting repeats the roughness of the brick. But there is a feeling of correctness about the whole combination, for the textures are selected and used in a natural

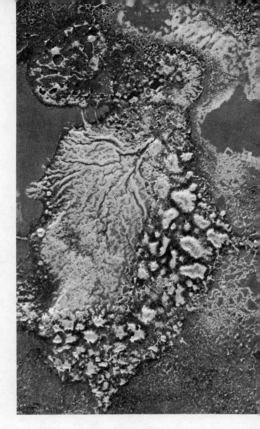

Fig. 7-25 Melted silver on copper creates an interesting texture. (Detail of a jewelry sculpture by Francis Stephen, Texas Tech University. Photograph by Randy Miller.)

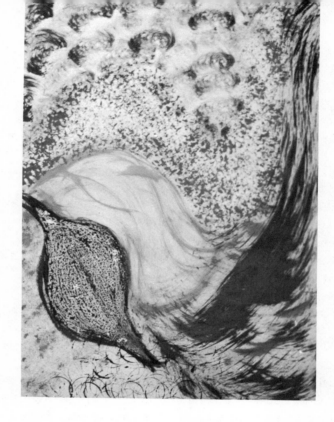

Fig. 7-26 A student problem in texture makes use of an oily background, twisted and stippled brush strokes, and dainty prints from the open end of a lipstick cover. (Student design.)

way to show off each of the areas to satisfaction. Textures should be selected for harmony of idea or for the use that is to be made of them rather than for their similarity or contrast.

CREATIVE EXPERIMENTS

1. Experiments to develop an awareness of textures:

    (a) Collect a group of actual textures and group in gradations of smooth to rough, thick to thin, heavy to light, etc. These might be all fabrics, or all leaves, or all pieces of bark, or whatever way you wish to collect and group them.

    (b) Collect a group of simulated textures from magazines or other sources and classify them in similar ways to (a).

    (c) Collect groups of textures which may be quite different (like

173

satin, fine kid, and pearls) but seem to have a natural affinity for each other or which we may associate together for a particular purpose.

2. Experiment with creating textural effects or compositions utilizing a variety of textures:

(a) Use finger paint and experiment with a variety of techniques of creating textural effects: with fingers, hand, arm, brush, palette knife, comb, sponge, wire mesh, and many other tools.

(b) Create an abstract collage of a variety of textures which harmonize or contrast satisfactorily with each other.

(c) Use different materials, such as clay, plaster, wood, moist sand, metal foil or leather, and shape, carve, or tool textural effects in the surface.

3. Experiment with planning designs inspired from natural textures in nature.

(a) Collect actual textures or photographs from magazines of textures, such as ice cubes in a beverage, moss on a rock, highlights and shadows on waves of water, folds in a glove, a bowl of vegetables. The number one can find is limitless to one with the imagination to see the design possibilities.

(b) Use any of the above to inspire one for a design for a stitchery or hooked wallpiece or rug, a blockprint, a collage, etc.

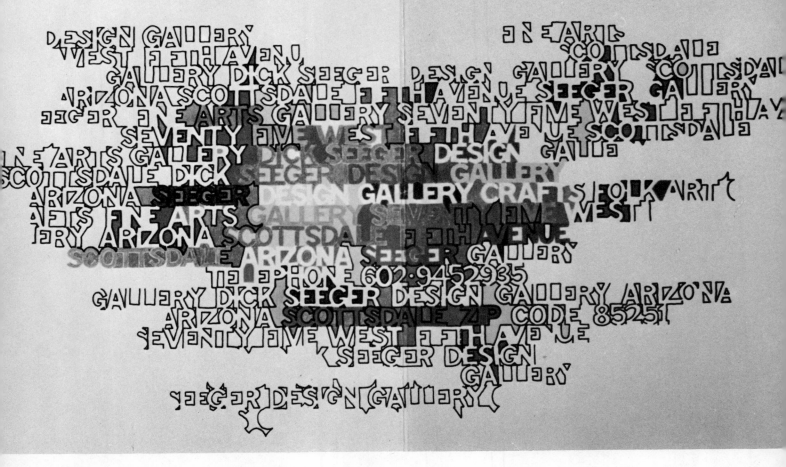

176

8

DESIGNING WITH THE ABC'S

The major purpose of this textbook has been to help you in your use of the principles of design to develop a more sensitive organization of the elements. For study purposes each chapter has centered around the use of the design principles mainly as related to one element. Your success or growth is reflected in your ability to combine these individual elements. Every time you make design judgments you reflect your understanding of design. You may choose to do a piece of sculpture, a painting, a piece of jewelry, design or even select an ensemble, design a piece of furniture, plan a room, or select an everyday object that you use.

A poster that you design will also show evidence of your sensitivity to design. Actually you can develop a poster with only a few simple technical skills. Through work with many students we have chosen posters as one way of looking at design understanding. This chapter dealing with lettering is planned to prepare you to develop a poster. Most college art departments offer lettering courses and this book is not intended to be a substitute for these courses. Skill and technique, produced by practice and study, are needed before you can become proficient in lettering.

Cave painting and hieroglyphics evidenced man's early desire to use a form of written communication. As man's society has become more complex, his need to rely on written communication has become increasingly important. An interesting discussion could be developed on the

Fig. 8-1 A catalog cover for Dick Seeger Design Gallery. (Designed by Jim Rapp.)

possibility that in the more advanced civilizations the need for written communication may have reached its peak and be ready to start a decline. What effect will the continuing advancement of audiovisual equipment and materials have on the need for the written word?

From the early drawings and symbols, our present-day written language has evolved. Although you have developed the written word to a point where you can convey ideas in various ways, by using an understanding of design you can increase your effectiveness in written communication. It is discouraging to receive a letter from a friend and not be able to decipher it. It is equally important to have written instructions or advertisements which are expressive. By applying our understanding of design, we will attempt to make our written words more communicative.

PRINTING VERSUS LETTERING

The organization of letters into words may be approached from two standpoints: that of *printing* and that of *lettering*. The first is a mechanical process in which the letters are set in type and printed by means of a printing press. This may consist of merely slipping rubber type, made in reverse, into grooves in a surface with a handle and using it as a "rubber stamp." The words on the stamp are pressed against an ink pad and then onto a paper surface. The paper takes up the ink from the stamp so the words can be read. Other printing processes deal with the preparation of plates for printing purposes, depending upon the kind of printing press to be used—letterpress or offset. The letters for composing the type are already designed, so it is a matter of deciding upon the size and style of type and the general organization of it for the printing plate.

Frequently we see on information cards or application forms the statement, "Please print." Actually, the words should read, "Please letter," because the hand process of shaping and composing letters is called *lettering*. We have become so familiar, however, with the term "print" to refer to a child's method of making his first letters that we still use the term incorrectly. Get into the habit of referring to printing as that which is done commercially with a printing press and lettering as that which is

Fig. 8-2 The word "HOPE" has been "letter-spaced" in each row with the height and thickness of the letters varied. This is easier to do with hand lettering than with type.

done by hand. We might also consider the hand-lettered art work from which a plate is made for printing purposes. See Fig. 8-1 for an example of this type of printing.

SHAPES OF LETTERS

RATIO OF WIDTH AND HEIGHT

Before we put letters together to make words, we need to study the basic *shapes* of letters. Each letter must be distinct and not easily mistaken for any other letter. It is fun to see what one can do to change the basic shape from a simple ratio of 2:3 (two units wide and three units tall), to a more unusual ratio of 2:5, 1:3, 3:7, 7:3, 3:2, etc. In these ratios the first number would indicate the width and the second number would indicate the height of the letter. Thus we could distort the letter to a tall, slender one, or a broad, squatty one (see Fig. 8-2). This distortion needs to be well done. If not, it will just look "arty," and is soon out of date. Decide carefully whether all capitals, all lower case, or a combination of capitals and lower case letters will be the best choice design-wise as well as for legibility.

FUNCTION

The prime purpose of all lettering is to be functional. When observed the lettering not only must be readable, but easily so. Many times when you are writing a theme you may spell incorrectly a simple word several times. But it may be difficult for you to discover this glowing error. The same thing holds true for your lettering. It is easy for you to read because you know what you intended to say. But can you still read it when it is "cold"? There is a story of a person who had written instructions for an employee. The employee failed to carry out instructions much to the dismay of the employer. The employee simply could not read the instructions and brought them back to this boss. The boss examined the instructions carefully for several minutes and replied, "I could read it if I could

179

remember what I had said." See Fig. 8-3. Does the lettering read "GRAY" or "G-RAY"?

CONSISTENCY

For lettering to be effective there must be consistency. Obviously in posters and advertising we break this consistency for certain words or phrases so they may draw special attention. (See Fig. 8-4.) However, this must be handled with care to keep from creating confusion. Variety in style of lettering and also variation in the size and placement may be planned to call attention to the main idea more effectively. In Fig. 8-5 note the placement of the first "d" in the word "middle" to emphasize the statement "How to end up in the middle".

The most obvious inconsistency in lettering is in the letter "I." In present-day lettering we have most often omitted serifs, commonly called "feet," except in the letter "I." If all letters carry serifs, then you have the beginning of consistency, but when you use these on only one or two letters, these letters tend to draw too much attention. Even so, there are times when consistency may be in conflict with functionalism. How would you letter the abbreviation of Illinois? In your own lettering, do you have a consistent placement of crossbars, as well as in your circles and straight lines? See Fig. 8-6. Note the inconsistency of the thickness of both vertical and horizontal parts of the letters in the word "LIFE."

Have you developed the best possible consistency for readability? Can you be objective about this? Or do you need someone else to examine your lettering?

CHARACTER AND PERSONALITY

Greater readability can be gained through the character or personality of the lettering. Uniqueness in lettering helps to draw attention, but in no way should it hinder the basic function. This individuality of lettering should be not only an expression of the individual but also the expression of what is being lettered. An example of this could be the personality of

180

Fig. 8-3 Care must be taken in planning the initial letter in a decidedly different style from the other letters of the word. It may make it difficult to read.

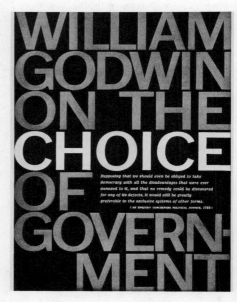

Fig. 8-4 Variety in the style of lettering and type as well as variation in size helps to call attention to the main idea. (Artist, Ed Kyser. Courtesy of Container Corporation of America.)

lettering used to describe a sheer fabric as compared to the lettering describing concrete. In Fig. 8-7 see the way in which the word "TORN" and "SOLID" are expressed with the irregular and smooth edges on the letters. In posters and advertising it is desirable for the important words, phrases, or thoughts to have a distinct character of their own. A headache remedy might emphasize the "splitting pain" of a headache as illustrated in Fig. 8-8.

SPACING OF LETTERS

MECHANICAL VERSUS OPTICAL SPACING

In lettering it is desirable to work toward similarity in proportions. However, you may create more design interest by introducing certain variations. Obviously, letters need to appear to occupy the same amount of space within each word. The word "appear" is the key to this thought. This refers to the problem of "optical" spacing, or using the eye to judge "equal" sizes of letters and amounts of space between the letters. "Mechanical" spacing refers to the use of a ruler to accurately measure heights and widths of letters, and placement of crossbars. This can be done more successfully for the guidelines for the top, bottom, and placement of the crossbars than it can for the actual width of the letters. We must consider the width of each letter, as well as the spacing of each letter in a word. If a "W" or "M" is made to occupy the same space as an "H," it would look crowded or pinched. It is equally difficult to have an "I" occupy the same space as an "H," much less an "M" or "W." Although these examples are more obvious, comparing an upper case "E" with an upper case "H" points out a more subtle point. The top, middle, and bottom of the "E" tend to lead your eye to the right, giving this letter the feeling of occupying a larger space. To make the "E" feel as if it occupies as much space as an "H," the "E" needs to be narrowed slightly.

From a design point of view, one cannot mechanically space letters successfully. There is no formula that can be applied to each letter. The space between an "A" and an "H" will be different than the space be-

Fig. 8-5 The emphasis centered on the first "d" because of its placement, variation of size, and darkness of value. (Photograph courtesy of Carrier Air Conditioning Corporation.)

Fig. 8-6 Inconsistency of thickness in vertical or horizontal parts of the letter leads to poor organization and appears to lack neatness. (Photograph by Randy Miller.)

181

tween an "A" and a "T." The "A" should actually extend under the arm of the "T." In most communities one is able to find signs that are mechanically spaced and difficult to read. Locally, one large sign says HOTEL. It actually reads as HOT EL.

Note in Fig. 8-9 how the "Y" in (a) appears smaller than the other letters, although each letter does occupy the same width space. In (b) the "E" has been made one half unit narrower and the "Y" has been made one whole unit wider, but all the letters appear to be more the same width. The spacing could still be improved by having a bit more space between the "G" and "R" and between the "R" and "E" to equalize the space between the open front of the "E" and the diagonal lines of the "Y." Sometimes it is even necessary to slightly "overlap" the upper and lower parts of diagonal line letters in order to create the optical illusion of equalized spacing. Note in Fig. 8-10b how the "A" and "Y" are spaced in this way.

Note the spacing in the word "LILAC" in Fig. 8-11. In (a) each letter occupies the center of each mechanically equal space. It gives the effect of too much space between the first "L" and the "I" and between the second "L" and the "A." In (b) the first "L" and the "I" have been placed close together while more space has been left between the "I" and the second "L," thus creating the optical illusion of equalized spacing.

In exploring variations in lettering it is important to be concerned with the placement of the crossbar. In mechanical printing processes the cross bar is usually in the center of the letter. This divides the space above and below equally. More interest can be gained by slightly raising or lowering this crossbar. Not only must we be concerned with the space a letter occupies, we must be aware of the spaces created within the letter, as well as the spaces between the letters.

Experiment with lettering the word "HAT." There are crossbars in both the "H" and the "A." More variation can be made in the placement of the crossbar in the "H" because of its vertical design. The "A," however, is limited in the placement of the crossbar in the middle or slightly below the middle for more pleasing proportions. Placement above the middle causes the design to appear crowded. More limitations arise as the diagonal sides of the "A" are made thicker and shorter.

Often in lettering we try experiments that fail to be effective. (This in no way means not to experiment because by no means are all experi-

182

TORN
SOLID

Fig. 8-7 The words take on personality or character to reflect the meaning of the word. For "Torn" the letters have literally been torn and for "Solid" the letters are heavy and bold.

Fig. 8-8 The "splitting" pain of a headache is expressed by a division in the tall angular letters.

Fig. 8-9 In A the letters each occupy the same amount of space, thus causing the E to look large and the Y to appear small. In B the E was reduced in size and the Y made larger to give a semblance of the same size.

Fig. 8-10 In A the same mechanical amount of space has been left between each letter, whereas in B the same optical space has been left, thus making it necessary to slightly "overlap" the Y over the A.

ments mistakes. Even when we analyze our errors we have the opportunity to learn.) To be different we sometimes try lettering that does not read from left to right, but from top to bottom or on a diagonal. Few words will read well up and down. In fact some well-known simple words become more difficult to read in this position. (See Fig. 8-12.) Even though the words may be more readable on a diagonal this should be used with caution. If these letters are out of balance they may cause one to assume awkward positions (consciously or unconsciously) in an attempt to recreate balance.

In recent years there has been marked improvement in the design quality of trade-marks and firm signatures. These show imagination, decorative letters, and symbols to personify the character of the firm represented (see Figs. 8-13a, b, c, and d).

TOOLS AND MATERIALS

Processes always affect the final product. Thus in our practical examination of lettering we need to take a look at the various tools and materials we may use to produce lettering.

When lettering, using a pencil, pen, or brush, it is important to be seated comfortably with both feet on the floor, with back straight, and

Fig. 8-11 In A the same mechanical amount of space has been left between each letter, whereas in B the same optical space has been left.

freedom of movement for your arm. Too many of us attempt to write with finger movement. Good lettering comes from good arm movement. Proper selection of materials, tools and the care of these reflect in your lettering. A pen point that is clogged with ink will produce sloppy letters. Expensive tools and materials are not necessary, but good selection is important.

Most professionals use guidelines to space the height of their letters. This may not be necessary, but it takes an outstandingly sharp eye not to use them. With uppercase letters, use two guidelines and with lowercase, use three. These should be drawn accurately with a ruler and very lightly so they can be removed easily.

When using drawing and inking tools, you should pull the point across the paper and not push it. When you push a tool the point tries to stab or become imbedded in the surface and it becomes difficult to produce a flowing line. With drawing and inking tools you should always pull the pen straight down or to the right. A left-handed person would pull the pen down and to the left.

Most students seem to prefer to start lettering with a pencil because this is a tool with which they are familiar. First, lay out guidelines for uppercase letters and use your pencil to produce the ABC's, striving for consistency and interest in your letters.

Which letters are made of all straight lines—vertical, horizontal, and diagonal? Which letters combine straight and curved lines? Which ones are made of all curved lines? It might be wise to start first with a page of practice strokes similar to those you will use later in your lettering. What difference will a hard or soft lead make? What effect can you obtain with the side of the lead? Now experiment with the lower case letters.

Pen and ink offer many possibilities in lettering. With the wide variety of pen points now being produced, you have unlimited possible designs for the individual letters. Before starting your page of ink lettering, practice first with the different types of strokes necessary for the various letters—vertical, horizontal, diagonal, and curved. Try each of them with different sizes and styles of pen points until you are sufficiently skilled to try the actual letters. Figures 8-14, 8-15, and 8-16 show the effect of three different kinds of pen points in several sizes; namely, the round nib, the square point, and the chisel point. Many of our new felt pens can be effectively used. These will not have the wide range of tips, but

Fig. 8-12 Readability has been reduced to a degree because one has to stop and spell the word in one's mind before reading it.

Fig. 8-13 *A*, an abstract symbol and monogram developed for the Trans-Mountain Oil Pipeline Co. (Designed by Walter Landor & Assoc., Industrial Designers, San Francisco, California.) *B*, emblem used by the Bozak Sales Company. The triangle symbolizes a loudspeaker, for which they are the dealers. (Photograph courtesy of Bozak Sales Company, Darian, Connecticut.) *C*, Computer Engineering Associates, Inc. of Pasadena, California use a simple monogram combined with an abstract symbol representing their firm. (Designed by Walt Landor & Assoc. Industrial Designers, San Francisco, California.) *D*, a simple dramatic lowercase "a" becomes the trade mark for the Ansul Chemical Co. (Courtesy of the Ansul Chemical Co., Marinette, Wisconsin.)

the ink that is dry when you put it on paper has certain advantages.

Brush lettering is basically similar to the pen except that there may be evidenced a more flowing line, and of course can be much larger. The chisel-shaped brush is still the one most used for lettering. Although the brush can produce wonderful effects, it takes much more practice to perfect one's skill with this tool. Furthermore, you need to keep in practice.

When experimenting with a complete word, remember to consistently vary the thickness of the vertical and horizontal parts and also watch the

Fig. 8-14 Using a round nibbed pen, fine or heavy, the letters become the same thickness throughout and have a rounded feeling about them. (Reproduced from the 17th Edition of Speedball Text Book, by Ross F. George. Courtesy of Hunt Pen Co.)

SINGLE-STROKE ROMAN

ABCDE
FGHIJK
LMNOP
QRSTU
VWXYJ
Z&R?ST

use the size of pen that will make the widest elements in one stroke

19

A

Style 'C' Speedball Pen Roman

A rapid legible alphabet for Artists and Sho-card Writers.

abcdefg
hijklmno
pqrstuv
wxyz&a
$12345¢
67890.

B

Fig. 8-15 *A,* a chisel-type pen is used for the above "Single Stroke Roman" lettering. The arrows indicate the direction of the strokes. The pen is always held at the same angle so the strokes are thick and thin. (Reproduced from the 17th Edition of Speedball Text Book, by Ross F. George. Courtesy of Hunt Pen Co.) *B,* lowercase letters to harmonize with the Single Stroke Roman lettering. Note the proportions within the letters so guidelines may be properly ruled. (Reproduced from the 17th Edition of Speedball Text Book, by Ross F. George. Courtesy of Hunt Pen Co.)

187

SQUEEZED HEADLINE
ABCDEFGIJL
KMNOPQRS
TUVWXYZ?
$123456789
AGHJKMNORSWXY¢

Fig. 8-16 By drawing the pen around each part of the letter, the stroke is the same thickness throughout. This technique may also be used to make the letters more broad than they are tall. (Reproduced from the 17th Edition of Speedball Text Book, by Ross F. George. Courtesy of Hunt Pen Co.)

HONOR

Fig. 8-17 Two widths of vertical parts used consistently, with even placement of the cross-bars in the "H" and "R." (Photograph by Randy Miller.)

Fig. 8-18 Placing the "E" backwards shows originality but makes the word more difficult to read.

Fig. 8-19 The left side of the "C" is thicker than the vertical parts of the other letters, but it creates the optical illusion of consistency, nevertheless. (Photograph by Randy Miller.)

optical spacing and placement of crossbars. Note in Fig. 8-17 the word "HONOR" has been planned so a consistent pattern of thick and thin verticals is evident without being monotonous. In Fig. 8-18 the designer strived so hard for originality in letter placement that it has an "arty" appearance and is difficult to read. In Fig. 8-19 the vertical thickness of the letters is not literally consistent because the left part of the "C" is much thicker than the right and left sides of the "O" and "B," but there still seems to be an impression of consistency and better optical spacing than there might have been if designed so literally.

Cut paper letters have some real advantages although it takes more time to make them than those made by other means. The major advantage is that your letters are glued down. This gives you an opportunity to cut all your letters and then arrange them. If any one letter does not work well, it can be discarded and a new one cut. Also if the word does not occupy enough space, the letters can be spread out. With drawing and inking tools, all your planning must be done first with no room for mistakes. With cut letters, later discovered mistakes can easily be corrected. There are many approaches to cutting letters. One method depends on folding, and another method on cutting all letters open (see Figs. 8-20 and 8-21).

Lack of space prohibits the showing of illustrations of folding and cutting each letter of the alphabet. But with a bit of experimenting, most students can discover ways of arriving at satisfactory proportions for cut letters. Once you have mastered the trick of cutting simple letters in which all parts of the letter are the same thickness, experiment with making variations in the thickness of the vertical and horizontal parts. Choose one letter, as in Fig. 8-22, and make each version of it a different design. Then choose one of those styles of letters and incorporate it into a complete word so that each letter in the word is made with the same style of letter.

The "rub-on letters" marketed under various trade names can be used by a person who does not have the technical lettering skills. Of course, sensitive judgment is needed, both in selection and placement of the letters. These letters have been effectively used for reproduction purposes. The "rub-on letters" are relatively expensive, but this is offset by the accuracy of shape and the ease of application. These letters lend them-

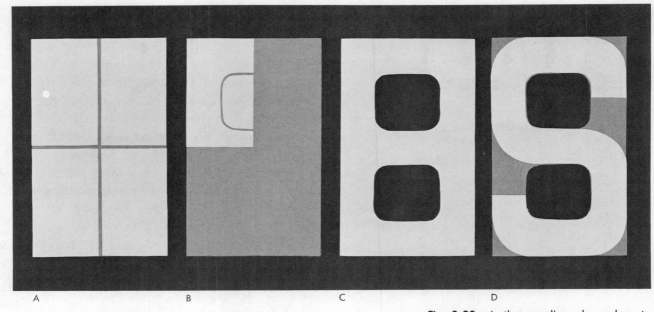

Fig. 8-20 *A*, the grey lines show where to fold the paper vertically and horizontally, *B*, the grey line on the left shows where to cut for a basic shape, *C*, the paper is unfolded to show the basic shape which results. Many letters may be cut from this shape, *D*, a letter "S" may be made from the basic shape by rounding the corners.

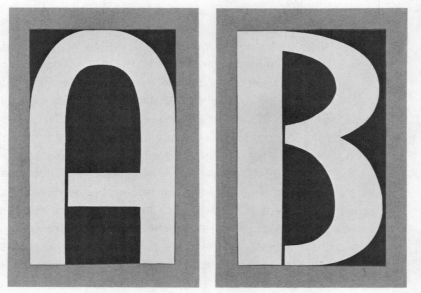

Fig. 8-21 Letters may be cut without folding, by cutting into a shape as indicated by the black lines. By this method, letters showing more variation in proportion may be cut.

Fig. 8-22 Experimentation with different styles of a single letter increases one's sensitivity for pleasing and unusual proportions.

Fig. 8-23 Varieties of type cut from magazines and organized give preliminary experience before planning a layout for a poster or other advertising.

selves to use in small scale and when limited numbers of letters are needed.

Designing with the ABC's can be fun, especially when one has developed sufficient awareness for beauty of shape, a sensitivity for pleasing spacing, and skill in representation with tools and materials available. Before beginning a plate of decorative lettering, one might experiment with organizing a page of interesting styles of type which express a pleasing unity in their shape (see Fig. 8-23). In Figs. 8-24 through 8-27 letters have been designed in a variety of ways for mottoes which become clever conversation pieces when framed and hung on the wall. Refer again to Fig. 8-1 in which lettering has been organized for a catalog cover design. It is true, the linear pattern is emphasized more than the letters and one must study the design to determine the exact wording, but in using letters as pure decoration, it is not always necessary to be able to read at a glance the individual letters or words. For instance, in the allover patterns developed from lettering in Figs. 8-28a, b, and c, the pattern is expected to be more important than the legibility of the letters. These might suggest allover patterns for wrapping papers or shopping bags for firms whose

191

Fig. 8-24 Mottoes give interesting word groupings for design experiments.

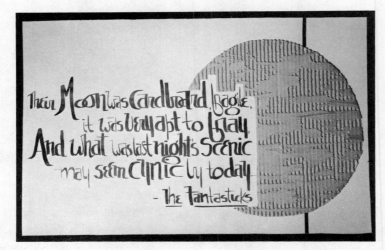

Fig. 8-25 Textures for background shapes add interest.

initials or firm names were repeated in the designs. This would serve as advertising and also lend a note of prestige to the packages carried out of the store.

With this variety of experience, you will be planning unusual lettering for your posters, bulletin boards, or display cases in a relatively short time. Even with limited skill, you need to develop design sensitivity in relationship to letters and lettering. Although this text has stressed that design tastes change, probably the change has been most apparent in our use of lettering. In the late nineteenth and early twentieth centuries highly ornate and decorative lettering was used. Later, lettering moved toward simplicity when sharpness and reading quality became of prime importance. Recently, more expressive quality of letters and lettering has be-

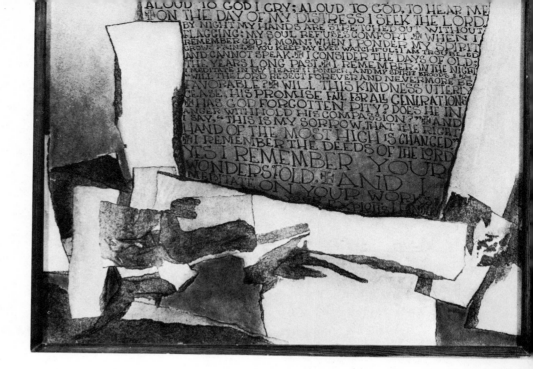

ALOUD TO GOD I CRY; ALOUD TO GOD, TO HEAR ME
ON THE DAY OF MY DISTRESS I SEEK THE LORD;
BY NIGHT MY HANDS ARE OUTSTRETCHED OUT WITHOUT
FLAGGING; MY SOUL REFUSES COMFORT WHEN I
REMEMBER GOD, I MOAN; WHEN I PONDER, MY SPIRIT
GROWS FAINT. YOU KEEP MY EYES WATCHFUL; I AM TROUBLED
AND CANNOT SPEAK. I CONSIDER THE DAYS OF OLD;
THE YEARS LONG PAST. I REMEMBER, IN THE NIGHT
WILL THE LORD REJECT FOREVER AND NEVERMORE BE
FAVORABLE? WILL THIS KINDNESS UTTERLY
CEASE, HIS PROMISE FAIL FOR ALL GENERATIONS
HAS GOD FORGOTTEN PITY? DOES HE IN
ANGER WITHHOLD HIS COMPASSION? AND I
SAY, "THIS IS MY SORROW, THAT THE RIGHT
HAND OF THE MOST HIGH IS CHANGED"
I REMEMBER THE DEEDS OF THE LORD
YES I REMEMBER YOUR
WONDERS OF OLD; AND I
MEDITATION YOUR WORK

Fig. 8-26   The lettering in the collage creates a pattern which is further emphasized by irregular dark and light shapes. (Designed by John Mahlmann, Texas Tech University. Photograph by Randy Miller.)

come important. Certain casual qualities and less tightness also have been seen. Presently, with the return of interest in the Art Nouveau style, often referred to as Nouveau Frisco, the highly ornate and decorative qualities are beginning to return. See Figs. 6-24, 6-25, 6-26, and 6-27. By the time this book is off the press other trends may be taking place. As designers, we not only should be excited by keeping informed concerning latest styles, but should be constantly striving to rediscover or discover new and different ways of designing with letters.

CREATIVE EXPERIMENTS

1. To develop an awareness for beautiful lettering and printing:

   (a) Find in magazines or newspapers examples of pleasingly proportioned letters—single letters, monograms or trademarks, whole words, as in "signatures" of firms.

   (b) Divide the examples in (a) into those which appear to have been

193

set up in type and those which were no doubt hand lettered before the plate was made for reproduction purposes.

2. To develop skill in designing with letters:

(a) Prepare a plate with a variety of guide lines showing different amounts of space between for various heights of letters. (1/8 inch, 1/4 inch, 1/2 inch, 1 inch.) Some rows of lettering might be provided with two guide lines for capitals and some with three for lower case letters.

(b) Using a pencil, and then your lettering pens, make a series of practice strokes of vertical lines, diagonals, and curves similar to those which you might use in making letters.

(c) Start lettering all the "straight-line" letters first (E, F, H, I, L, T); next do the ones with diagonal lines (A, K, M, N, V, W, X, Y, Z); lastly do the ones with a combination of straight and curved lines (B, D, G, J, P, R, U): and the all-curved ones (C, O, Q, S).

(d) After you have developed sufficient skill in making capitals in a variety of proportions (tall and thin, short and wide, two-thirds as wide as tall) practice making lower case letters (also in a variety of proportions).

(e) Plan a plate in which you choose one letter and practice varying the proportion of the letter in as many ways as you can. Use this letter in a five or six letter word, making the word occupy the same amount of space each time, but vary the proportion of the letters and the spaces between.

(f) Plan an allover pattern using a group of letters as the decorative motif which is repeated for the pattern.

(g) Choose a poem or a motto and arrange it on a plate in a pleasing manner.

(h) Choose one letter and cut it in a variety of proportions. Arrange them on a page in an interesting way.

(i) Choose one word (four or five letters) and cut the letters so one arrangement of the letters has been made using tall, thin letters, and the other arrangement uses broad, squatty letters.

(j) Choose one word that suggests a certain personality or character. Cut letters which reflect this personality.

Fig. 8-27 A serigraph designed by Sister Mary Corita of Immaculate Heart College makes dramatic use of letters to carry a message. (Owned by Bill C. Lockhart.)

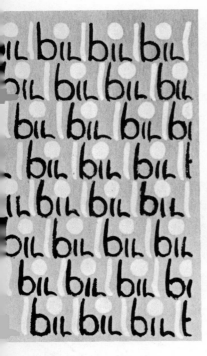  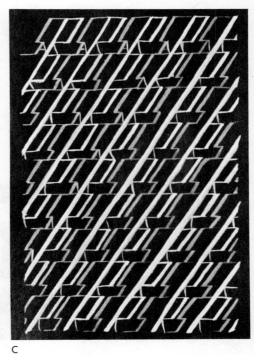

B   C

Fig. 8-28 *A, B, and C. Letters arranged as allover patterns may be used satisfactorily for fabric patterns or gift-wrapping papers.*

196

9

DESIGN SPEAKS OUT

For the purpose of study you have been introduced separately to the elements of design: line, shape, space, color, and texture. This individual examination was planned to help you to become better acquainted with and to develop a greater sensitivity to each design element. However, in design or in a particular design each element must be viewed in its interrelationship to other elements. One design may depend mostly on line, but for the design to have quality the spaces between the lines must be examined. Thus the element of space has entered. Also contrast between the line and background must be present for the lines to be visible. This contrast may be in color, (hue, value or intensity), in texture, or in a combination of these. Therefore, the success of a design cannot rest independently on any one element but on the sum total of those used.

Your understanding of design depends on your knowledge and skills in using the guideposts of design to achieve the best organization of the design elements. When you work with design you are placed in the position of combining the design elements. However, we have selected posters as a project which lends itself easily to the combining of your design knowledge and skills.

Fig. 9-1 The letters are changed in size to fit the spaces in between other letters, expressing the idea of ''crowding'' more into the space than one would normally do. (Photograph courtesy of McKelvy's Furniture, Inc. and Byrd Advertising Agency, Lubbock, Texas)

197

PURPOSE OF A POSTER

What is the purpose of a poster? The basic purpose can be described as being the communication of information. This information may be further described as the expression of a product, a service, or an idea. What ways are available for expressing information? The poster may be dependent on *lettering* that clearly expresses or communicates information. This may best be seen where the lettering dominates and is easily read. At one time we talked about posters that could be read by someone who is running.

Some posters depend on *illustrations* to communicate. This may be seen in travel posters where the illustration of a country, mountains, or seashore is more important than the lettering. The illustration becomes the selling point. See Fig. 9-1 in which both lettering and illustration work together to communicate the "out of space sale." Other posters may depend on *decorative quality*. This is especially true of the psychedelic posters. These use lettering, but the communication develops from the decorative quality or overall effect and not from the readability of the letters. Note the posters illustrated in Figs. 6-24 through 6-27. They are planned especially to make it necessary for the viewer to pause and study the design to decipher the wording and the entire composition if he wishes to get the full significance of the idea expressed. In Fig. 6-24 the colors are full intensity, a double complement of red and green, orange and blue, vibrate and make the message difficult to read. However, the general division of space, distortion of the letters, and dramatic treatment of the illustrations hold the attention long enough for us to grasp the full meaning and significance. In Fig. 6-26 the single hue of red-violet is contrasted in value by the neutral black, but the letters are so distorted to emphasize the decorative quality that it becomes necessary to guess what some of the letters are. In this case the distortions and decoration do have certain communicative values, even when the lettering is difficult to read. Figure 6-27 also stresses the purely decorative quality in a highly rhythmical and exciting use of reverse values of red and green. Some contemporary paintings are difficult for the average layman to understand at first glance, but their unusualness may eventually seem most exciting and demanding of one's attention. Note in Figs. 9-2 and 9-3 the designs of

(left)

Fig. 9-2 Simplicity and irregular gradation of size of the shapes of the geese lend an exciting rhythmical character to the poster in which illustration dominates. (Student design.)

(right)

Fig. 9-3 Elimination of much of the figure of the crow lends a dramatic air of mystery to the poster in which the illustration is made more prominent than the lettering. (Student design.)

the geese and the crow predominate with the lettering subordinated. In Fig. 9-4 the lettering is given a decorative quality and distorted to fit the torso shape of the background. In each case the lettering or the illustration has been given a decorative quality to make it attract and hold the attention of the viewer. In Fig. 9-5a and b the comparison is shown of an inadequate and a more satisfactory arrangement of type. In (a) all the main information is made the same size type so it is not especially evident that the card is advertising greeting cards. In (b) the words, "Unusual Greeting Cards, Come—See—Select" are in bold type to easily communicate the message.

In recent years we have begun to be more aware of the fact that posters can truly be works of art. Toulouse-Loutrec's posters are hung in museums and are valued for their art quality. Today more and more reproductions of posters reflecting aesthetic quality are being used in our homes. Travel posters, with the emphasis on illustration, are being matted and hung in our homes and offices. At one time these were collected by

199

Fig. 9-4 The silhouette of the torso is made a mere background for the decorative letters which are shaped to fill the space and attract one's attention. (Student design.)

travelers for pleasant reminders, but today they are mass produced for the general public. The psychedelic posters are being used for their decorative qualities and are available across the country.

Whichever form of communication a poster may take, the quality of the poster depends on the organization of the design. Figs. 9-6 and 9-7 express good art quality in the organization of posters. Each has a dramatic quality of simplicity with strong contrasts of dark and light. Formal or informal balance can be equally effective. Thus "design speaks out" through posters.

200

DEVELOPING A POSTER

In developing a poster, you must start with the information you wish to communicate. As an example we could use an announcement that appears on most campuses.

> The Freshman Class with the cooperation of the Student Union will have an all-freshman dance. This affair will be semiformal. No admission will be charged. A college group of musicians, The Campus Combo, will provide the music. This dance will be held in the Student Union Ballroom on Friday, November 13, from 8:30 until 11:00. This is a stag or drag affair.

How can you most effectively communicate this information with a poster? Should you emphasize lettering that is easily read? Should you use illustrations that reflect the information? Should you use decorative quality of lettering? Illustration may well reflect the qualities of the dance. However, this takes certain drawing skills which all students will not have. With illustration, too much detail and realism will often detract. Design quality should take precedence over realism. Simplification, distortion, or other changes in illustration may make it more effective. Often it has been said you should strive to get the most impact by the simplest means. The design must attract the attention of the passerby, but also hold the attention long enough so he will read what you tell him and have him act accordingly. This means that the poster should have influence. (This point is one to ponder. Our department owns a number of psychedelic posters; many of these we enjoy and only a few have we really bothered to read! The influence, then, would be an aesthetic one.)

If you are advertising a dance, the poster should help put the viewer in a mood for dancing, make him want to go. Needless to say, with the abundance of advertising today, the poster must be especially strong to earn attention. If you are advertising a delivery service, you need to plant the idea so that the viewer will call you when he has need of this service. If you are urging people to stay off the grass, your method of expressing this idea should be strong enough so the viewer will be inclined to stay on the sidewalk. One university put signs such as "Don't walk on us; we're trying to grow." Each sign was different and somewhat humorous, causing the viewer to want to read it. These could obviously be more effective

Fig. 9-5 In A only the firm name is empha-sized. In B other subordinating words, such as "Invite You," "Unusual Greeting Cards," and "Come, See, Select" are also emphasized because of the size of the type. (Photograph courtesy of Design Today, Inc., Lubbock, Texas.)

than "Keep Off The Grass." At one time Burma Shave used this effectively in their signs along the highways.

Only simple skills are needed to make lettering stand out and be effective. These skills can be reasonably controlled by most students in a short period of time. The poster design may be more effective when lettering receives more emphasis than illustration. However, each of you needs to make your own decision. With your skills and ability, which approach will you use to best convey the information concerning the freshman dance? One caution, by attempting to convey too much informa-tion, you may lose all communication. Sometimes we hear long-winded

Fig. 9-6 Formal balance has been planned by means of a bisymmetrical vertical balance. The horizontal balance has been planned by uneven distribution of dark and light with the smaller area of dark at the bottom. (Artist, John Massey. Courtesy of Container Corporation of America.)

203

Fig. 9-7 A dramatic, informally balanced distribution of dark and light. (Artist, W. H. Allner. Courtesy of Container Corporation of America.)

speakers who ramble on and on. Later, we may fail to remember a single point. One poster we viewed had 157 words, all with practically the same emphasis. Remember, he who says too much, says nothing.

By expressing only two or three points about the freshman dance, what would you choose as being of first importance? Of secondary importance? Do you need to say that all freshmen are invited to the freshman dance, or does freshman dance imply this? Maybe other words will be more effective than "dance." What are some of these? This suggests another

204

point. Who will be your audience? What are the different characteristics of your group? How much should these differences be considered in the designing of a poster? Would a poster that advertises a carnival for the elementary school students, for high school students, and one for college students be different? Some would say, "No," because all of us become youngsters when involved with a carnival. However, it becomes obvious that with many activities the interest of our audience will vary greatly.

In the chapter on lettering we have talked about personality of letters. For any poster, it is important to use lettering that characterizes the information. Would there be a difference in the lettering used to tell about a new exciting perfume and the excitement of a circus? There are no set rules that will tell you what lettering to use. Each of you must decide on lettering that will best carry your information. How would you personify letters to carry best the information for our dance poster?

Posters affect the viewer's feeling-responses. If they are crowded, this same feeling can be conveyed to the observer. Note again in Fig. 9-1 letters are changed in size to fit the spaces between other letters, expressing the idea of "crowding" more into the space than one would usually do. Sometimes a disturbing factor may result in persons subconsciously rejecting the information. On our campus a series of posters became the focus of editorials and letters to the editor of our student newspaper. The extremely brilliant color combinations seemed to produce a strong bilious feeling in the audience. Is it possible for a poster to be extremely disturbing and still be successful?

Variety must enter into your poster; how much depends upon your interpretation of the information. The greater the variety, the greater the dramatic quality. Our present generation has practically been reared on variety—especially in advertising. Neon signs, flashing lights, weird and noisy sounds, movement in the form of flapping plastic flags, pinwheel swirls, electric vibrations to create movement, and changing patterns of depth in a composition as the viewer moves, all add to the variation to call our attention to some form of advertising.

How long the poster will be posted may have bearing on the dramatic quality of the poster. How dramatic should your dance poster be? How much variety in size and shape should you work toward? Consider the variation not only in lettering but in other shapes and illustrations. What colors should you select for the poster? If the dance had been given a particular theme, such as Western, Parisian, or Spring, would this affect your color choices? How much variety do you need in hue, value, and intensity? Should various textures be included? What textures lend themselves to your dance?

What materials should you use? Slick paper, rough paper, fabrics, yarns, and sandpaper are only a few of the many textures that may be successfully introduced into posters.

Should your poster be flat or three-dimensional, or a combination? The answer to this and other questions should be based on one point. What will make the poster most effective with the most eye appeal? This will require originality on your part. Just being different will not necessarily make your poster good. Use your guideposts to good design as your final evaluation. Even the most simple poster becomes very complex when viewed from all points of design. However, the more effectively you use design, the more the design will speak out for you.

In the preceding paragraphs concerning the poster for the freshman dance, you have been asked leading questions pertaining to:

1. The lettering versus illustration and decorative quality.
2. The readability.
3. The audience who reads the poster.
4. The personality of the letters.
5. The viewer's feeling-responses.

Study the four ski posters shown in Figs. 9-8a, b, c, and d. Note in (a) and (b) the lettering has been emphasized because of the size and simplicity, contrasts of dark and light, and minimum number of words used. In (c) the word "SKI" has been developed into a clever and graceful pattern of ski trails that will attract the attention of the viewer. In (d) the wording is complicated because each word at the top of the poster is in a different style of lettering. The value contrast of the word "Skiing" is not strong enough to attract attention. The space occupied by the two areas of lettering and the illustration are all approximately the same. There is competition between the lettering and the illustration so that it

Fig. 9-8 In A and B the wording has been emphasized because of the size and the stark simplicity of the rest of the poster areas. In C the word "SKI" is developed into a pattern suggesting trails to attract attention. In D too much variation in both the lettering and the illustration compete for attention.

A

B

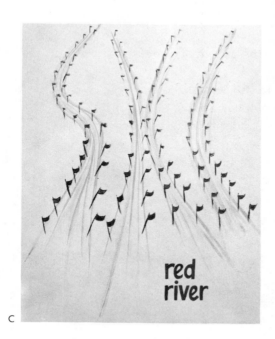

C

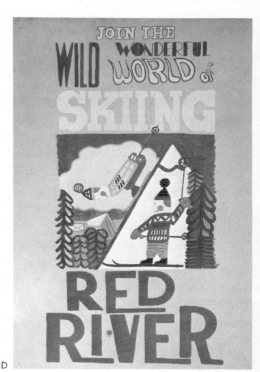

D

is difficult to grasp the message at a glance, as one can easily do with each of the other three posters.

Following are a number of points to remember in planning a poster. Glance occasionally at these same ski posters plus the others in the chapter to check how many have been applied.

POINTS TO REMEMBER IN PLANNING A POSTER

1. Keep it simple.
    (a) Don't try to say too much in one poster.
    (b) Don't try to say too much in one space.
2. Have either lettering or illustration dominate rather than compete for attention.
3. Select letter styles to harmonize with the idea of the poster. Execute them neatly, even though they may be greatly distorted to fill a particular space.
4. Select hues to harmonize with the idea of the poster.
5. Use strong contrast of values for better carrying power at a distance.
6. Plan a variation of sizes of letters and/or background areas, but don't arrange them in stair-step fashion.
7. Remember that strength and stability are gained through repetition, but don't overdo it and give a restless, monotonous feeling.
8. Use strong movement, perhaps by means of diagonal lines—but not from corner to corner.
9. Add a note of humor, if possible.
10. Group words that make sense together.

Write	Write Letters Home	Write
Letters Home	Daily	Letters Home Daily
Daily		

Not: Write Letters
   Home Daily

CREATIVE EXPERIMENTS

1. To develop awareness of well-designed posters or advertising:

   (a) Find examples of posters or advertising which depend mainly on illustration for their effectiveness.

   (b) Find examples which depend mainly on wording for their effectiveness.

   (c) Find examples where the total effect of the poster or advertisement reflects the personality or character of the product, service, or idea.

2. To experiment with creating a poster:

   (a) Choose a product, service, or idea which could be expressed by means of a poster.

   (b) Make several thumbnail sketches of layouts for your poster.

   (c) Select the layout which seems to have the best design possibilities, and select the tools and materials which you wish to use for the poster.

   (d) Now construct the poster.

   (e) Evaluate the poster according to the principles of design.

10

THE END AND THE BEGINNING

The last chapter of the book is obviously "The End," but what is meant by "The Beginning"? This book is planned to help you, as a consumer and/or designer, develop design knowledge and sensitivity. An organization for the study of design has been presented. Where you go now depends on you. Every day of your life you will be expressing your personality through the things you choose and creating things that will reflect your design awareness and your taste. The changing nature of our times brings about changes in our design concepts. The study and reexamination of design must continue for each of us, because there is no point of arrival or stopping place.

The rest of your life you will be constantly faced with design decisions. Your better decisions will be reflected in the richness of your life. As you become more sensitive to color variations, textures, and other design elements you become more "in-tuned" to environment.

We hope you will continue to grow in both design knowledge and sensitivity—thus, "The Beginning."

EVALUATION

Fig. 10-1 The stacks of chairs may give one inspiration for an exciting pattern for use in many ways. (Courtesy of Knoll Associates, Inc.)

Our ability to evaluate design is a reflection of our sensitivity. What new ideas should we look for in designs? Recently a Sunday supplement

211

Fig. 10-2 Carved wooden bird. Note the harmony of the grain lines with the contour of the sculpture. (Owned by Mrs. Ethel Jane Beitler.)

carried a full-page advertisement of modern electric ranges. Two of these ranges showed pleasing proportions, sharp clean lines and reflected honest use of today's materials. The third was a poor copy of an old wood-burning stove. It was made to look like the old cast iron stove with tall legs, yet the top burners and oven were electric! We might add that we hope the designer of the last range has continuing nightmares! This becomes our "value judgment." So it is important to look at criteria that are used in our evaluation.

HONESTY

Honesty in use of materials is one evaluation point. What is meant by this? Is each material used in its natural way? Is metal used as metal, wood as wood? Does the use of materials reflect honesty? Each material

212

has certain natural qualities. The same is true of an individual. As individuals, we function best when we are what we are—not pretending to be something else. A fourteen-year-old girl with bright lipstick and high heels pretending to be a woman of the world fools no one. Honest use of materials is best expressed when a material is not made to pretend to be something it is not. Figures 10-1, 2, and 3 all gain as designs by honest use of materials. The exposed metal of the stacking chairs in Fig. 10-1 create an honest decorative effect and displays the structure of the chair. The pattern of the wood grain in Fig. 10-2 enhances the beauty and grace of the bird and base. The scrap iron in Fig. 10-3 which shows the use of the cutting torch and welding helps express the "Hooded Owl." Honest use of materials enhances the overall quality of each piece we design.

EXPRESSION OF TODAY

Another evaluation point is how well the design reflects our present knowledge and the use of modern tools, equipment, and materials. By today's standards you will find examples of excellent furniture design constructed many years ago.

There is no intention of questioning the value of antiques; however, the production of earlier designs with today's skills, tools, and equipment is highly questionable. You may see a silver bowl that has been spun on a lathe, and then has been hammered to show the hammer marks as if the metal had been raised by a silversmith. If the bowl is spun on a lathe, or stamped in a press, why attempt to hide the process? No matter what method, there is still the obligation of developing the best design possible. Often with our students, we have them visit the variety store to discover inexpensive, mass-produced examples of good design. Our students are always amazed that excellent design may still be purchased for only a small amount.

Mass production has given us many luxuries we could not otherwise have. However, we must be careful not to consider all mass-produced articles as poor design.

The true test of art is how well it reflects today's times. It is always

Fig. 10-3 Marks of the cutting torch and welding on the scrap iron for the "Hooded Owl" express honesty in use of materials. (Designed by Dr. Foster Marlow, Head of Department of Art, Southwest Texas State College.)

Fig. 10-4 Industrial buildings which reflect today's time may stimulate creation of exciting designs. (Parking building in Dallas, Texas. Photograph by Don Murray.)

difficult to evaluate what does reflect today, and it is much easier to evaluate art of fifty years ago. The mechanical age has given way to the atomic and space ages; yet, we are still surrounded by industry. The shapes seen in Fig. 10-4 may stimulate exciting designs, and at the same time be devoid of human quality. The mass of people in the stadium, the cars, and roads (Fig. 10-5) may reflect similar qualities. Our mass production, our crowded cities with the slums, housing developments, and the freeways are some of the things that make up the everyday lives of millions of people. How does today's art reflect this? Could psychedelic, "pop," and "op" art be a protest for a return of emphasis to the individual?

Even if we as authors had clear-cut answers for today (which we don't), each day's changes must cause us to constantly search for new answers. Whichever design we select or choose, we may ask the question, "Is this a reflection of today?"

INDIVIDUALITY OF THE DESIGN

In evaluation of design, you should look for individuality of the designer. This may be referred to as the *originality* of the design. Without this uniqueness, any design loses much of the design quality—whether it be a painting, a building, or a mass-produced item that falls into a sameness.

214

Fig. 10-5 The mass of people in the stadium, the cars and roads give inspiration for today's designs. (Photograph courtesy of the Lubbock Chamber of Commerce.)

At the same time, just because a design is different there is no assurance that it will have design quality.

One sculptor uses a severe test. On the completion of a piece he asks himself—could anyone else but I have done this? He feels only when he has produced a piece that truly reflects his personality and his experiences that he succeeded. One artist has said that we are always trying to improve on the quality of other artists. But, unless we do improve or enrich earlier designs, we have failed to grow or add to our environment. So, whether you are selecting or producing your own design you need to evaluate its individuality.

ARRANGEMENT OF DESIGN ELEMENTS

How well the various design elements are organized into a pleasing whole is obviously an important point to evaluate. The overall arrangement of the various parts may be simple when the best combination of elements are present. For example, you might first evaluate how well the various textures of the many materials relate to each other. You may have the right combination of textures, but how do the colors affect the textures? What effect do the various shapes have on the textures? The mul-

215

tiple relationship between the different elements becomes very complex. The wallpieces in Figs. 10-6 and 7 are examples of aesthetic quality achieved through sensitive arrangement of design elements. Even in black and white, the patterns of light and dark give indication of the color harmonies present. There is no mechanical way of arriving at the most pleasing combination. Admittedly it is most difficult to evaluate a design that is almost right in application of design principles, lacks character, says nothing, and shows little imagination or vitality. However, when the best arrangement is achieved in connection with (1) honesty of materials, (2) expression of today, and (3) individuality of the design, an overall aesthetic quality is usually present.

CREATIVE PROBLEM SOLVING

As a designer you should be constantly faced with achieving new and exciting results. When faced with a new and different design solution, there are certain "birth pains" that take place. In fact, the first solution is usually slow in taking place, but on the way to completion of the solution other solutions may come to mind. So constant practice in designing, and redesigning, is one of the best ways to keep your designing skills and abilities sharp. We recognize that the more skilled or talented may come to a solution quickly, while others may have beginner's luck. However, we encourage our students to bring several solutions to any one problem. The first solution may not be the best—in fact when you keep pushing for several solutions, the later ones are apt to be the best. Either way, the more solutions you discover, the better opportunity you have of growing and of selecting the best one.

FRESH POINT OF VIEW

As we grow in design ability we must constantly look for new or fresh inspiration. Obviously, our basic inspiration comes from our personal experiences and our awareness. Our personal experiences are the sum total of our interactions with others and our environment. However, it

Fig. 10-6 Combination of weaving and braiding techniques in passion pink, orange, and purple yarn. (Made by David B. Van Dommelen, Associate Professor, Pennsylvania State University.)

Fig. 10-7 Aesthetic quality is achieved by a sensitive arrangement of the elements of design. (Photograph courtesy of Mrs. Lila Kinchen, owner; designed by Ethel Jane Beitler.)

becomes important to increase our awareness. This means not only looking, but seeing; not only touching, but feeling, and developing overall understanding and empathy. All of us pass through a very exciting world every day of our lives, but are we really aware of what is around us? Recently a gentleman had a photograph made of his home for use on a Christmas card. When he viewed the photo, he was amazed to find that the bricks were indented under the windows. Of course, he had only lived in his home for 15 years. This man had normal vision, but he had not seen. How do we learn to see?

First, we must take time to look. A friend who lives in the Sun Valley in Arizona has commented on the view of the distant mountains. She has told us how exciting the mountains are because they never are the same. Not only do they change every hour of the day, but they are different from day to day. Although this person is not an artist in the traditional sense; she has learned to see and become aware of the subtle changes. So if

217

we will take even a few minutes each day to relook at something we know, we will enrich our sensitivity.

It becomes important, not only to relook, but to find a different point of view. It is easy to become excited when looking at a familiar landscape from the air. A city, farm land, mountain, or desert takes on an entirely different feeling when seen from above.

It is a revelation the first time you fly over a drab city that you know well. The distance minimizes the trash and litter of the industrial area and gives it a cleaner and more unified pattern. The rows of houses, with their sidewalks, driveways, and streets make exciting designs. As long as we limit ourselves to only a narrow point of view, we limit our own design solutions.

Many times we discover design inspiration from a common object when viewed through a microscope. This might be called "taking an inside look." The roots of a strand of hair, a drop of water, or many common objects become interestingly different when magnified, or even when viewed under polarized light.

Often, taking a child's point of view will give a different look. One time in class we had the college students describe and draw a design laboratory. The students had complained about the small drawing tables and the lack of space in the laboratory. A five-year-old child was turned loose in the room. He was able to run under the drawing tables. He later described the huge room and the large tall drawing tables. He said the bottom of the drawing tables were filled with gum. This young child gave all of us a new look at our room.

Force yourself to take a different view of known things. How about a worms-eye view. His surroundings, which will be the same as yours, take on drastic and dramatic differences.

How do you normally view a tree? If the distance is great, you may never see the tree for the forest. If you move in close, you become aware of the *tree*. Yet, if you come in even closer, you may become aware of the *bark*, a *twig*, or a *leaf*. The close view of the piece of wood in Fig. 10-8 evidences cracks and textures that most people never see, much less become aware of as inspiration for design.

As a designer, we also need to be concerned with feeling and mood. How does the tree change in early morning light? in the rain? in the cold

Fig. 10-8 Take a close look at a piece of wood to see evidence of cracks and textures which could give inspiration for designs. (Photograph by Randy Miller.)

Fig. 10-9 The minute "dove of peace" in a sand dollar is actually only one-fourth inch in width, and yet, when magnified, can give excellent design inspiration.

winter? or with a strong wind? or late at night? How does the bark feel when it is wet? or cold? How does the tree smell when freshly cut? when it is dry and musty? when it burns? When the tree is cut, how does the grain pattern look? Few people are aware of the miniature "dove of peace" (Fig. 10-9) found inside the sand dollar. The texture of the sponge in Fig. 10-10 offers exciting patterns and textures, if we are willing to "see." In Fig. 10-11 we see the organic pattern created by the torch's flame directed on styrofoam. Not only does this open design possibilities of the material (styrofoam), but suggests patterns that could be used in other designs.

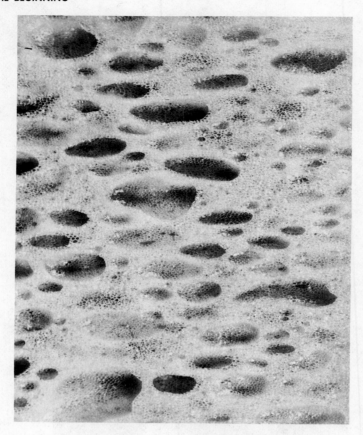

Fig. 10-10 The various sized holes in a sponge offer pleasing design possibilities.

Additional design inspiration is available if we are willing to take a fresh point of view.

UNUSUAL PROBLEMS

Many times we open up new avenues for designing when we set up an unusual problem. One painter we know will take a certain size canvas for a series of paintings; then he will drastically change the shape to a long thin, or a square, and sometimes irregular shape. By varying the shape on which he paints, he feels that he forces himself to look for new solutions.

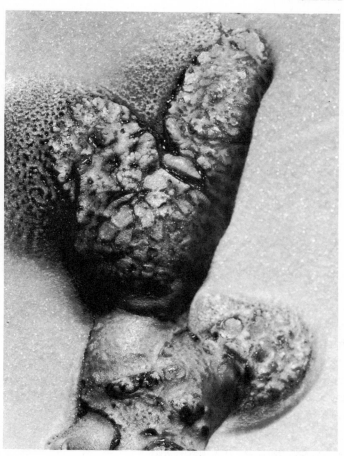

Fig. 10-11 An organic pattern created by the torch flame directed on styrofoam produced delightfully strange design ideas.

An interior designer sometimes discovers new, exciting design solutions when faced with an unusually shaped room. Maybe it is long or the ceiling is very high. This forces the designer into a different approach. The selection and arrangement of furniture in a normal room may have to be abandoned in an unusual size or shape. Even faced with the problem of combining old furniture with new furniture in a room creates a different approach.

Suppose you basically prefer to work with flat surfaces, painting or advertisements; then create a different problem by facing a three-dimensional sculpture problem, or a window display. Thomas Hart Benton often made three-dimensional clay figures for the figures he planned for his painted murals. This was done so he could study the light and shadow to obtain greater naturalism. But any designer who will develop different or unusual problems is further developing his sensitivity and skills.

Necessity has been identified as the mother of invention. So, as a designer, deliberately look for unusual design problems. By this we mean unusual for *you*. What about designing a new and different automobile or a better telephone?

If you want to grow in your design ability, make yourself face as many unusual design problems as you can. Whether your solutions are practical or not, you will be growing.

INVOLVEMENT IN PROBLEM

What has involvement to do with solving a design problem? The late Viktor Lowenfeld, who was a distinguished art educator, used the expression "identify with their work" in relation to children. The terms "identify" and "involvement" are closely related.

How do you become involved in a design problem? The portrait painter may be using an elderly man as a subject. The painter works at understanding the old man and puts himself in place of his subject. He has a better chance of catching the mood or feeling. What kind of life has the man lived? What excitements has he faced? What disappointments? What is his outlook? What does he believe? The more sensitive you become to your subject, the greater the identity you establish.

Suppose you have selected an industrial theme for a design. You will need to gain knowledge, understanding, and sensitivity for your subject. Maybe you have developed sensitivity to the shapes and colors.

Of course, this involvement could also be involvement with the materials. You might prefer to get acquainted or to know the materials. It is important for the designer to know the "characteristics" or qualities of material. You need to know what a material will do—how suitable the material is for a design.

Throughout history birds have served as themes for the artist. The wall

222

plaque in Fig. 10-12 was inspired by the artist observing sparrows. He became fascinated by watching them as they searched for food in the yard around his studio. The commercially produced pigeons in Fig. 10-13 from Mexico reflect the designer's involvement in the decorative pattern inspired by the bird's feathers. In Fig. 10-14 the artist was involved with the feeling of graceful flight.

Fig. 10-12 The ceramic wall plaque was inspired by observing sparrows in the artist's yard. (Designed by Mr. Franz Kriwanek, Head, Department of Art, University of Delaware.)

Fig. 10-14 The artist observed birds in flight and chose welding rods for his material to design a better feeling of graceful flight. (Designed by Dr. Bill C. Lockhart.)

Fig. 10-13 Commercially produced Mexican bird forms on which the painted decoration was inspired by observing the pattern of the bird's feathers. (Owned by Dr. Bill C. Lockhart.)

NEW SOLUTIONS

"New solutions" is related to the new use of old materials as well as the use of new materials. One danger a designer faces when he gains certain skills and knowledge of a material is that he may stop experimenting. To keep growing you must continually strive to take a new look at your materials. This experimentation helps to find different qualities in a material. Very few designers have explored the full possibilities of any materials. So whether it be paint, fabric, or metal, take time to relook.

In an age when technical advances are being made so fast, it is difficult to keep up with new materials, tools, and equipment. When the acrylic paints were first introduced they were used as oil and as watercolor. Only when experimentation took place did some of the qualities of the acrylic begin to develop. At times it is easier to be creative with a new and unknown material. As an explorer facing a new material you have no known guidelines or limitations. You must experiment. Students who have inhibitions or fears of paint may work with materials in a three-dimensional design without these fears. When you work with a material that is new to you, you will probably be freer to take a new look.

Alex Osburn coined the phrase "brain storming," which could apply well to solving design problems. This is a process used with groups and individuals. You first define the problem and then begin looking for as many solutions as possible. During this searching it is important not to be critical—or attempt an evaluation. This criticism must come later; if it comes too early you limit the number of possible solutions.

Suppose we have a problem of designing dinnerware. First, let us look at possible solutions. We may improve the structural and applied design. Does a plate need to be round or square? So often in eating on a conventional plate you reach over part of your food. What about a long narrow plate so that all of the food could be in a row?

It is important here to point out, again, that at first don't say this solution won't work. Don't worry about evaluation until all possible solutions have been made.

We can look for different materials to use for the dinnerware. What different clays might be used? Would plastic or metal work? Or even design a plate that may be eaten to save washing dishes! This sounds ridiculous, but look at the ice cream cone.

After exploring, you begin to evaluate—try and discard. This same process would apply to the design of a rug or a painting. Students, too often, will turn in one design for a project. Suppose the problem is to design a wallpiece. You may first make not one, but many small sketches. Then you select several and spend the time redesigning these. You might even use tracing paper—changing shapes and sizes to achieve a more pleasing arrangement.

Or you might start by looking at what materials are available, which combination of materials would work. This could be collage, carving, printing processes, as well as unlimited others. The appliqued crab in Fig. 10-15 produced by the natives of the San Blas Islands, while not necessarily a new solution, shows how fabric and thread are used for a design statement. The designer probably chose the "crab" as the motif for his work. The crab in Fig. 10-16 represents a different approach. The artist collected a variety of "found objects," then let these objects suggest his solution. The railroad spikes for legs, the monkey wrenches for pinchers,

Fig. 10-15 Cutting fabrics and appliquéing them for a crab shape requires careful planning to solve the design problem in a pleasing manner. (Applique from the San Blas Islands.)

the nails for feelers, and the body became a new solution, where the crab was inspired by materials. The designer must constantly look for new solutions to old problems.

SUMMARY

This chapter is planned to show ways of developing further sensitivity and skills in designing. Where you go depends on you. We strongly feel that the more sensitive you become, the richer life you will lead. This does not mean sensitive only to aesthetic values, but to the creative side which must be interwoven with aesthetic qualities. Your aesthetic and creative abilities must be used and you must continue your development. If these qualities lie dormant and are not used, they may slowly fade away. So we truly hope this is "The Beginning."

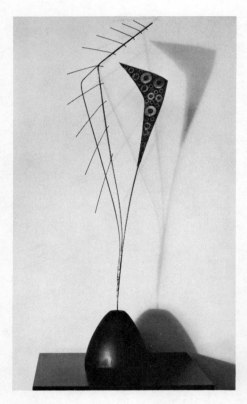

Fig. 10-16 Found objects may suggest a new solution to a design problem. ("Crab" designed by Dr. Foster Marlow, Head, Department of Art, Southwest Texas State College.)

Fig. 10-17 Steel, wire, and washers welded together to give a flexible movement in space. (Designer, Bill Lockhart; owner, Martye Poindexter.)

226

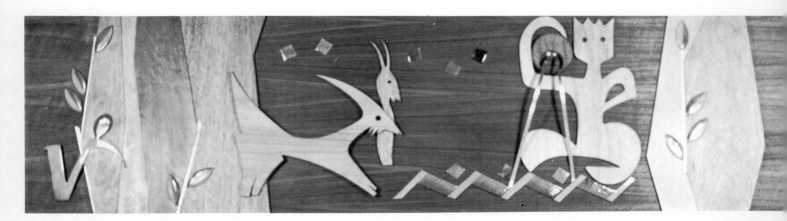

Fig. 10-18 Zodiac signs in poplar on walnut and mahogony backgrounds with bright spots of color added in bits of enamel-on-copper. (Design by Ethel Jane Beitler. Photograph courtesy of Design Today, Inc.)

BIBLIOGRAPHY

Adams, Edward, George Pappas, and David Van Dommelen, *Design At Work: It's Forms and Functions,* Pennsylvania State University Center For Continuing Education, 1961.

Albers, Joseph, *Interaction of Color,* Yale University Press, New York, 1963.

Anderson, Donald M., *Elements of Design,* Holt, Rinehart, and Winston, New York, 1961.

Bates, Kenneth F., *Basic Design,* The World Publishing Co., New York, 1960.

Bawr, John, *Nature in Abstraction,* Macmillan Co., New York, 1958.

Bayer, Herbert, Walter Gropius, and Isa Gropius, *Bauhaus: 1919–1929,* Museum of Modern Art, 1938.

Beitler, Ethel Jane, *Create With Yarn,* International Textbook Co., Scranton, Pa., 1964.

Benedicks, Huldt, *Design in Sweden Today,* Swedish Institute for Cultural Relations, Bonner, Stockholm, New York.

Bevlin, Marjorie Elliott, *Design Through Discovery,* Holt, Rinehart, and Winston, New York, 1963.

Birren, Faber, *Creative Color,* Reinhold Publishing Company, New York, 1961.

Blassfeldt, Karl, *Art Forms in Nature,* (photos, examples from plant world), E. Weyhe, New York, 1929.

Cataldo, John W., *Graphic Design,* International Textbook Co., Scranton, Pa., 1966.

Cheney, Sheldon, *Story of Modern Art,* Viking Press, New York, 1950.

Collier, Graham, *Design Books: Form, Space, and Vision, Discovering Design Through Drawing,* Prentice Hall, Inc., Englewood Cliffs, New Jersey, 1964.

BIBLIOGRAPHY

Emerson, Sybill, *Design, A Creative Approach*, International Textbook Company, Scranton, Pa., 1953.

Faulkner, Ray and Sarah, *Inside Today's Home*, Holt, Rinehart, and Winston, New York, 1960.

Faulkner, Ziegfeld, and Hill, *Art Today*, 4th Ed., Holt, Rinehart, and Winston, New York, 1963.

Feldman, Edmund Burke, *Art As Image and Idea*. Prentice Hall, Inc., Englewood Cliffs, New Jersey, 1967.

Goldstein, Harriet and Vetta, *Art in Everyday Life*, 4th Ed., The Macmillan Co. New York, 1940.

Gottshall, Franklin, *Design for the Craftsman*, Bonanza Books, New York, 1967.

Grillo, Paul Jacques, *What is Design?* Paul Theobald and Company, Chicago, 1960.

Haggar, R. G., *A Dictionary of Art Terms*, Oldbourne Press, London.

Hastie, Reid and Christian Schmidt, *Encounter With Art*, McGraw-Hill Book Co., New York, 1969.

Itten, Johannes, *The Art of Color*, Reinhold Publishing Corp., New York.

Jacobson, Egbert, *Basic Color, An Interpretation of the Ostwald System*, Paul Theobald, Publisher, Chicago, Ill., 1948.

Judd, Deane B., and Gunter Wyszeski, *Color in Business, Science, and Industry*, John Wiley and Sons, Inc., New York and London, 1963.

Kainz, Louise and Olive Filey, *Exploring Art*, Harcourt Bros., New York, 1947.

Karlsen, Tredemann, *Made in Denmark*, Reinhold, New York.

Kepes, Gyorgy, *The Nature of Art and Of Motion*, George Braziller, New York, 1965.

Kepes, Gyorgy, *Structure in Art and in Science*, George Braziller, New York, Vision Value Series, 1965.

Kepes, Gyorgy, *The New Landscape in Art and Science*, Paul Theobald Co., Chicago, 1963.

Kepes, Gyorgy, *Language of Vision*, Paul Theobald Co., Chicago, 1951.

Krevitsky, Nik, *Stitchery: Art and Craft*, Reinhold Publishing Corp., New York, 1965.

Laury, Jean Ray, *Craze for Color*, Reinhold Publishing Corp., New York, 1965.

Lowry, Bates, *Visual Experience*, Henry N. Ambranes, Englewood Cliffs, New Jersey, 1961.

Moholy—Nagy, Laszlo, *Vision in Motion*, Paul Theobald Co., Chicago, 1947.

Moholy—Nagy, Laszlo, *The New Vision*, Wittenborn, Schultz, New York, 1947.

Moseley, Johnson, and Koenig, *Crafts Design*, Wadsworth Publishing Co., Inc. Belmont, California, 1963.

Munsell, A. H., *A Color Notation*, Munsell Color Co., Inc., Baltimore, Md. 1941.

230

Nelson, George, *Problems of Design,* Whitney Publishers, New York, 1957.

Randall, Reino, and Edward C. Haines, *Bulletin Boards and Display,* Davis Publications, Inc., Worcester, Mass., 1961.

Rowland, Kurt, *Looking and Seeing, Series I: Pattern and Shape, II, The Development of Shape, III., The Shapes We Need, IV., The Shape of Towns,* Ginn and Co., Ltd., London, 1964.

Schinneller, James, *Art: Search and Self-Discovery,* International Textbook Co., Scranton, Pa., 1961.

Seiberling, Frank, *Looking Into Art,* Holt, Rinehart, and Winston, New York, 1959.

Thomajan, P. K., *Handbook of Design and Motifs,* Tudor Publishing Co., New York, 1950.

Warner, Esther S., *Art: An Everyday Experience,* Harper and Row, New York, 1963.

Wesley, Arthur Dow, *Composition,* Doubleday Doran and Co., New York, 1941.

Wolchovak, Louis, *The Art of Three Dimensional Design,* Harper and Bros., New York, 1959.

Wolchovak, Louis, *Design For Artists and Craftsmen,* Dover Publications, New York, 1953.

GLOSSARY

TERMS PERTAINING TO DESIGN

Abstract. Portraying a basic shape without imitating appearances. The shapes may be simplified, exaggerated, or rearranged.

Aesthetic. Pertaining to beauty, taste, or the fine arts; artistic. Appreciating or loving the beautiful.

Applied Art. A phrase often used to describe those arts which are made by craftsmen.

Asymmetric. Not symmetrical. Usually much more free than formal balance. Also referred to as occult, or informal.

Balance. A principle of design which presents an impression of equal distribution of weight in a design.

Baroque. A type of late Renaissance art which was a reaction from standardized classic forms in the direction of greater freedom. Baroque art is often characterized by strong contrasts and elaborately twisted and curved forms.

Biomorphic. Forms related to life or living organisms, such as a bean or a pear.

Bisymmetrical Balance. Identical elements or powers of attraction placed equally from the center of a design.

Bizarre. Strikingly out of the ordinary or out of keeping, especially as to fashion, design, color and the like.

232

Calligraphy. Beauty of lines, varying in widths, curve, rhythm, etc.

Cartoon. A comic drawing. It may be satirical in nature. It may also be an artist's drawing to serve as a model for a fresco, mosaic, tapestry, etc.

Character. In art, character refers to individuality, creativeness, or a satisfying expression of imagination.

Classic. Belonging to the culture and art of the ancient Greeks and Romans.

Collage. An organization of elements in a semiflat abstract manner. It is mainly an experiment in combination of textures.

Composition. The product of an arrangement of related parts; design, organization.

Congruity. Harmony of the various parts or elements of design with the whole.

Continuity. An orderly sequence of the parts of a design from one to the other and to the whole.

Contour. The line bounding a shape or form; outline.

Decorative Design. The design which is added to the surface of a structural design for the purpose of enriching it.

Design. An organization of the elements of design with two aims, order and beauty.

Diagonal. Oblique—expressing motion or a bracing effect against an opposite force.

Dimension. In art in general: any measurable extent, as breadth, length, or thickness. In color: a property or characteristic, such as hue, value, or intensity.

Distortion. A change from normal proportions. A twisting or writhing motion or misshapen condition.

Dominance. Superiority in size, placement, or general character.

Dynamic. Giving an effect of movement, energy, force.

Eclectic. Selecting and combining from various doctrines, systems, or styles that which is thought best. Most of our present-day houses which were built twenty-five or more years ago are eclectic; borrowing from such historic examples as the Colonial, French Provincial, or Tudor.

Elements of Design. Tools and materials to use in making a design. The elements of design are: line, shape, space, color, and texture.

233

Elevation. A drawing showing no perspective, but is a flat view, of the front, side, or rear of an object.

Emphasis. A principle of design which leads the eye first to the most important part of a design and to all other parts in the order of their importance.

Exotic. Belonging to another part of the world; foreign; strange.

Expressionism. Art in which the emphasis is on inner emotions, sensations, or ideas rather than actual appearances.

Fashion. The prevailing mode; manner of doing a thing.

Form. In art, a three-dimensional object.

Formal. Made or done in accordance with regular or established forms and methods, or with proper dignity and impressiveness; orderly.

Formal Balance. Organization of identical or similar elements or powers of attraction placed equal distances from the center so there is equal distribution of weight on both sides.

Free-Form. Shapes or forms which do not follow any set of rules; biomorphic.

Geometric. Characterized by regular lines, curves, and angles, as in geometry.

Good Taste. Application of the principles of design to the problems in life where utility and beauty are considerations.

Graphic Processes. Those processes for printing or reproduction of drawings, photographs, etc.

Grotesque. An unnatural but decorative combination of human and animal forms interwoven with plant forms; also applied to art forms which are awkward or incongruous.

Harmony. The resulting attribute when the principles of design present an impression of unity with sufficient variety to add interest.

Horizontal. Parallel to the horizon; suggests or conveys a feeling of repose.

Impressionism. A movement in art, particularly painting, in which the aim was to preserve the vividness and force of the first impression nature makes on the painter's vision and to convey the sensation of movement and light. Impressionism is often associated with artists such as Seurat, Manet, Monet, who used broken color in small dots or brush strokes which blended together in the eye of the observer.

Informal Balance. Organization of unlike elements or powers of attraction placed unequal distances from the center of a design so there is equal distribution of weight on both sides. Sometimes referred to as occult or asymmetrical balance.

Isometric Drawing. A drawing in which no attempt has been made to show true perspective, but lines have been made parallel and at right angles to each other.

Layout. A term used in printing and in commercial art referring to the arrangement of pictures and words on the page.

Lettering. The process of making letters by hand with pencil, lettering pen, etc.

Linear. Pertaining to or composed of lines. Very narrow and long.

Mechanical Spacing. Spacing which is measured with a ruler or other mechanical means.

Medium. The material used to produce an art object. Also the liquid which is used to mix pigments to make them suitable for painting. Also the middle value of gray on the standard value scale.

Mobile. A three-dimensional abstraction which usually hangs from the ceiling and has moving parts which rotate as the currents of air strike them.

Montage. A picture or page arrangement made by grouping or superimposing several pictures so as to blend into one another, or so as to show figures upon a desired background; a composite picture; also a process of composing a picture.

Mosaic. A type of inlaid decoration, composed of small pieces of stone or glass, generally used for the decoration of walls and floors, but recently used for table tops.

Motif. A distinct principal idea or element of design.

Mural. A painting or decoration on a wall.

Nonobjective. Referring to painting and sculpture which are expressions in pure form and design showing no resemblance to natural objects.

Objective. A goal; that toward which effort is directed; an aim; an end.

Opposition. Diametrical differences in position—variation in direction of lines.

Optical Illusion. An unreal image seemingly presented to the senses; any misleading appearance; false perception.

Optical Spacing. Spacing which is measured by the eye as a gauge.

Organic. Having the character of living forms. Organic art, such as the houses of Frank Lloyd Wright, shows the vitality and unity found in animals and plants.

Organization. The systematic relation of parts to each other and to the whole; design.

Pattern. Anything shaped or formed to serve as a model or guide in forming something else. Any decorative design, usually in a planned repeat.

Perspective. The art of representing, by a drawing made on a flat surface, solid objects or surfaces conceived of as not lying on that surface; representing objects as they appear to the eye. The art of conveying the impression of distance and depth.

Picturesque. Having a striking or irregular beauty, quaintness, or charm.

Pigment. Any coloring material, but usually dry earth mineral, or vegetable compound, which is mixed with a liquid to produce paint.

Plane. Any flat or uncurved surface.

Plastic Elements. Line, shape, form, space, color, and texture; the elements of which all products of the plastic and graphic arts are composed.

Precept. A working rule or law.

Principles of Design. Guideposts to use in evaluating the organization of the elements of design. The principles of design are: balance, proportion, emphasis, and rhythm.

Printing. The act of reproducing a design upon a surface by means of any graphic process.

Proportion. A principle of design which deals with the relationship between each part of a design in relation to each other and to the whole design.

Psychedelic. A color experience denoting a high mental state, an intensely pleasureful perception of the senses, aesthetic entrancement, and creative impetus. Frequently considered a color experience induced by hallucinatory drugs.

Radiation. Lines or parts of a design growing out of, or extending from, a line or a point.

Realism. The representation of things as they are in life without idealizing them.

Renaissance. The great revival in art and learning in Europe beginning in the fifteenth century in Italy. The Renaissance began in Italy and quickly spread to the other countries of Europe. Artistically, it involved the rejection of the Gothic style and the revival of the classical Roman style and ideas.

Repeat. A term used to denote one complete unit of a repeated design.

Representational. Characterized by a likeness to or depicting persons and scenes as they exist, without any attempt at idealization.

Rhythm. A principle of design which provides an easily connected path over which the eye may travel.

Rococco. A type of Renaissance ornament developed during the seventeenth and eighteenth centuries in which rocks and rock like forms were combined with fantastic scrolls, shells, etc., to present a lavish display of decoration, more graceful than baroque.

Scale. The size of the parts in relation to the whole object or a representation of an object to the object itself.

Sculpture. Figures or arrangements of forms carved, cut, hewn, cast, constructed, or modeled in wood, stone, clay, metal, plastic, or other material.

Shape. A two-dimensional flat object.

Simulate. To assume or have the mere appearance or form of, without the reality; imitate.

Stabile. A three-dimensional abstraction which has no moving parts like a mobile.

Static. At rest or in complete equilibrium; suggesting no movement; opposite to dynamic.

Still Life. A painting of objects, such as fruits, flowers, vases, etc., as distinguished from those of landscapes or people.

Structural Design. The design made by the size, shape, color, and texture of an object, whether it be the actual object or a representation of it on paper.

Subordination. To hold of less importance; minor.

Surrealism. A type of painting in which the artist paints the images from the subconscious self rather than what he sees about him. Surrealism is an attempt to go beyond actual observation, and paintings are likely to be full of symbolism. Dreamlike.

Symbolic. Representation by symbols rather than by imitation.

Symmetry. A balancing of parts in which those on one side of the center are the exact reverse of those on the other. Formal balance.

Tactual. Pertaining to the sense of touch.

Technique. Method or way of doing something, such as the way to hold a brush or the amount of pressure to place upon it to make particular types of strokes.

Tempera. Opaque water color, or an opaque paint in which the pigment is mixed with an albuminous substance, frequently white of egg rather than oil or water.

Tension. Any strained relations. Tensions in art are the representations of the pulling forces between parts of the composition.

Texture. Surface characteristics.

Tonal. The general color scheme or collective tones of a picture or composition.

Traditional. Handed down from one generation to another; still having usefulness.

Transition. Leading the eye easily from one part of a design to another. Growing out of it.

Unity. Similarity. Of equal importance. Oneness.

Vertical. Standing erect—suggesting upward force.

Void. Empty; free; producing no effect.

TERMS PERTAINING TO COLOR

CLASSES OF COLOR

Acid Colors. Cool colors, such as cyan-blue, ultramarine, magenta, which we associate with the color of acids.

Advancing Colors. The warm colors, or those of bright intensity that seem to advance.

Cool Colors. Cool colors are those which have blue in their mixture, as green, blue-green. Violet is on the borderline between warm and cool.

Earth Colors. Colors, such as ombre, yellow ochre, mustard, terra cotta, which are found in the earth's strata.

Intermediate Hues. A mixture of one primary and one secondary. Yellow-green, blue-green, blue-violet, red-violet, red-orange, and yellow-orange are the six intermediate hues.

Normal Hue. The pure color; the brightest intensity that it is possible for a color to be.

Popular Hue. A name given to a special value or intensity of a color by a manufacturer for the purpose of "popularizing" it for a particular product, season, etc.

Primary Hues. The basic colors from which are derived all the other colors. Red, blue, and yellow are the three primary hues.

Receding Colors. The cool colors or the ones which are grayed in intensity seem to recede.

Secondary or Binary Hues. A mixture of two primary hues. Green, orange, and violet are the three secondary hues.

Standard Hue. The six major hues on the color wheel: red, yellow, blue, green, orange, and violet.

Warm Colors. Warm colors are those which have red in their mixture, as red-orange, orange. Yellow is sometimes considered a warm hue because of its association with sunshine.

COLOR HARMONY

Colors used together for a particular purpose and giving the impression that they belong together.

COLOR THEORY

An arrangement of colors for the purpose of study.

Chemist's Color Theory. A color system that studies color from the chemical properties of pigments as used for dyes and paints.

Munsell Color Theory. A color system consisting of five primary hues (red, blue, yellow, green, and purple); and five secondary hues (yellow-red, green-yellow, blue-green, blue-purple, and red-purple).

Ostwald Color Theory. A color system which assumes, through psychological testing, that there are six basic color sensations. These are black and white (achromatic sensations), and four chromatic sensations of yellow, red, blue, and seagreen with the complementary hues opposite each other. A total of 24 hues make up the complete wheel.

Psychologist's Color Theory. Studies color from the way it affects the mind and emotions.

Physicist's Color Theory. Studies wavelengths and intensities. Light theory.

Physiologist's Color Theory. Studies color from the way in which it is received by the eye. Fatigue experiments.

Prang Color Theory. One of the color systems. Three primary hues (red, blue, and yellow); three secondary hues (green, orange, and violet); and six intermediate hues (yellow-green, yellow-orange, blue-green, blue-violet, red-violet, and red-orange).

COLOR WHEEL

The arrangement of colors in their correct order in relation to their mixtures. The complements are opposite to each other, the line connecting them going through the center of the circle.

CONTRASTING HUES

Hues which have no color in common, such as blue and orange.

CONTRASTING INTENSITIES

Some bright and some dull intensities used together.

CONTRASTING VALUES

Values which are not near each other on the value scale.

DIMENSION OR PROPERTY

The three characteristics or ways in which colors differ: hue, value, and intensity.

Hue. The name of the color, such as red, green, blue-green.

Intensity. The brightness or dullness of colors.

Value. The lightness or darkness of colors.

GRADATION OF HUE

Closely related hues which show a gradual change from one hue into another; such as yellow, yellow-green, green, blue-green.

GRADATION OF INTENSITY

Closely related intensities which show a gradual change from one intensity to another; as bright, slightly grayed, moderately grayed, dull.

GRADATION OF VALUE

Closely related values which show a gradual change from one value into another; such as high-light, light, low-light, medium.

HIGH INTENSITIES

Hues which are bright in intensity; normal, pure pigment.

HIGH VALUE

A value above medium on the value scale.

LOW INTENSITIES

Hues which are dull in intensity; have been grayed considerably.

LOW VALUE

A value below medium on the value scale.

LOWER THE INTENSITY

To make duller; add the complement or a neutral.

LOWER THE VALUE

To make darker in value; add black or more pigment.

MAJOR CONTRAST

Large interval, strong contrast.

MECHANICAL COLOR COMBINATION

Colors selected from a mechanical arrangement on the color wheel, not necessarily harmonious with each other until the values, intensities, and amounts are taken into consideration for the purpose for which the colors will be used.

Analogous. Neighboring or adjacent hues, related, having a color in common.

Complement. The color opposite another on the color wheel, the line connecting the two going through the center of the circle, as red and green.

Double-Complement. Combinations of two hues with their corresponding complements, such as yellow-orange and yellow-green with red-violet and blue-violet.

Monochromatic. The use of one hue in a variety of values.

Split-Complement. Combinations of a hue with the hues on either side of its complement, such as yellow with red-violet and blue-violet.

Triad. Use of three hues which are equally distant on the color wheel, such as red, yellow, and blue.

MINOR CONTRAST

Small interval, closely related, similar.

MISCELLANEOUS COLOR TERMS

Color Path. A series of colors showing a gradation in one or more dimensions.

Dissonance. A satisfactory use of reverse order of values; like a minor key in music.

High Key Colors. Those colors which are normally light in value, or those which have been raised in value to those above medium on the value scale.

Law of Areas. Large areas should be quiet in effect with small areas showing strong contrast of hue, value, or intensity.

Low Key Colors. Those colors which are normally dark in value, or those which have been lowered in value to those below medium on the value scale.

Natural Order of Values. Hues selected in the same order of values as the normal equivalents are found on the standard value scale. For instance, normal green is the equivalent of low-light, whereas normal blue-green is the equivalent of medium. Whenever these two hues are used together and the green is lighter than the blue-green, they are said to be in the natural order of values.

Neutral. Gray, black, or white.

Neutralize. To gray, or dull, or lower the intensity of a color by the addition of the complement or a neutral.

Pastel. A value lighter than the normal in a grayed intensity.

Reverse Order of Values. Contrary to the order of values of hues as the pure pigments are shown on the standard value scale. For instance, normal green is the equivalent of low-light, whereas normal blue-green is the equivalent of medium. When blue-green is made lighter than the green they are in reverse order of values.

Saturation. Full strength of pure pigment.

Shade. A value of a color darker than the normal.

Spectrum. The band of successive colors which appear when a ray of sunlight is passed through a prism, breaking up the light into a sequence of strong colors.

Tint. A value of a color lighter than the normal.

Tone. The prevailing effect of a color brought about by blending.

NORMAL VALUE SCALE

The steps on the standard value scale from white to black, with the normal hues placed in relation to their equivalent values.

RAISE THE INTENSITY

To make brighter; add more pure pigment.

RAISE THE VALUE

To make lighter in value; add white or water.

RELATED HUES

Several hues which have a hue in common, such as yellow, yellow-green, and green all have yellow in common.

RELATED INTENSITIES

Intensities which are similar—all bright or all grayed.

RELATED VALUES

Values which are close to each other on the value scale.

STANDARD VALUE SCALE

The steps of dark and light between white, seven values of gray, and black.

VALUE KEY

A system or series of values based on their relation to a dominant value.

High Major Key. If there is an interval of five or more steps between the darkest and lightest values, strong contrast results, and it may be called a high major key if there is a larger area of light value than dark.

High Minor Key. If the darkest and lightest values in the design are no more than three steps apart, it may be called a high minor key if they are all values above medium on the value scale.

Intermediate Major Key. Strong contrast of values with a larger area of medium value (a value from the middle part of the value scale).

Intermediate Minor Key. Closely related values all low-light, medium, or high-dark.

Low Major Key. Strong contrast of values with a larger area of dark value than light.

Low Minor Key. Closely related values all below medium value.

INDEX